THE MORALITY GAP

*An Evangelical Response to
Situation Ethics*

THE MORALITY GAP

*An Evangelical Response to
Situation Ethics*

13691

by

ERWIN W. LUTZER

MOODY PRESS
CHICAGO

Library of Congress Catalog Card Number: 72-77957

ISBN: 0-8024-5603-0

All scripture quotations in this book are from
The New Scofield Reference Bible, unless indicated otherwise.

Printed in the United States of America

To

my parents, whose lives illustrate that love can be served by obedience to biblical commands. "And this is love, that we walk after his commandments" (2 Jn 6).

Contents

5

ACKNOWLEDGMENTS

The author thanks The Westminster Press for granting him permission to quote from the following books:

From SITUATION ETHICS, by Joseph Fletcher, The Westminster Press. Copyright © MCMLXVI, W. L. Jenkins.

From MORAL RESPONSIBILITY, by Joseph Fletcher. Copyright © MCMLXVII, The Westminster Press.

From HONEST TO GOD, by John A. T. Robinson. Published in the U. S. A., 1963, by The Westminster Press. © SCM Press, 1963.

From THE SITUATION ETHICS DEBATE, edited by Harvey Cox. Copyright © MCMLXVIII, The Westminster Press.

Thanks also to Zondervan Publishing House for permission to quote from ETHICS: ALTERNATIVES AND ISSUES by Norman Geisler, Copyright © 1971, by Zondervan Publishing House.

6

Foreword

THREE THINGS CAN BE SAID for this book.

First, it is interesting. No one will fall asleep reading it.

Second, and more importantly, no one can miss the author's point. Some authors get so technical that they lose not only their readers, but also themselves in their own analytical machinery. Here the line of argument is as easy to follow as Interstate 70.

Third, and most important of all, the problem is one of the most pressing, most acute, and most tragic phenomena plaguing Americans today. A cult of antimorality is destroying society. Immorality in all ages has destroyed individuals; but now so many individuals are being ruined, that a nontotalitarian republic is becoming an impossibility.

This antimoral movement is not completely unorganized and spontaneous. Every social movement of like dimensions must have spokesmen with a rationale. One of the most popular exponents of contemporary depravity is Joseph Fletcher, professor of biomedical ethics at the University of Virginia School of Medicine. Note that not only secularists such as Hugh Hefner of *Playboy* are attacking morality. But as with the ecclesiastics and the Popes of the Middle Ages, who were often the most depraved, so now the ecumenical churches are leading in advocating abortion and adultery.

The present volume draws an accurate blueprint of Professor Fletcher's thought and shows just how his right angles are actually obtuse. More literally stated, Mr. Lutzer's analysis of Fletcher's arguments reveals that they are a combination of two mutually exclusive principles, plus dependence on the impossible calculations of Jeremy Bentham. That Fletcher should try to present his immorality as Christian ethics may at first astonish the reader, but he will see the consistency when he learns that Fletcher approves and advocates hypocrisy and deception.

A personal word. It is a pleasure to write the foreword for the first publication of one of my students. During my college days, Francis L. Patton was in old age; B. B. Warfield died; Robert Dick Wilson had only a few more years. Conservative scholarship, with very few exceptions, seemed near total eclipse. Today, however, I can name over five hundred college and seminary professors who hold that the Bible alone and the Bible in its entirety is the Word of God written, and therefore inerrant in the autographs. Now appearing in print is Erwin Lutzer, a young scholar, who, I trust, will stimulate a hunger and thirst for righteousness and for scholarship too.

GORDON H. CLARK

Preface

ONE MAN does not steal because he believes in the universality of biblical morality. Another man might not steal merely because he is afraid of being caught or because he believes that stealing would not result in the greatest good for the greatest number—at least in *that* situation. Outwardly, both men have the same conduct, yet the reasons for their conduct are so different that it would be a mistake to assume that they had the same moral philosophy.

In ethics it is not sufficient merely to agree on a given moral decision. The *reason why* we reject certain forms of conduct and accept others is just as important as the conduct itself. In some cases, those who advocate the new morality make moral decisions which are in harmony with biblical commandments; but this superficial similarity should not blind us to the fact that such agreement is only coincidental, perhaps accidental.

Those who read this book with this explanation in mind will understand why I totally reject situationism, even though in certain instances the situationist may happen to approve of moral decisions which are consistent with biblical morality. The assumptions of biblical morality and situationism are so diverse that superficial agreement should not obscure the radical difference between the two.

1

The Morality Gap

IN CHICAGO a business firm entitled "Term Paper Research, Inc.," is open for orders. Charging $3.85 per page, the agency guarantees that experienced researchers will write term papers for college students who discover near the end of the semester that they possess more cash than ambition. A student who hired the firm to write one of his term papers was asked whether the practice should be considered immoral. His answer: "No. Each student has to evaluate his priorities; if he has more important activities to do, then having someone do his term paper is not wrong."

In Los Angeles a group of businessmen and their wives gather for a party every Saturday evening. Before all leave for home, the names of the wives are placed into a hat and passed around the room. That evening each man goes home with the wife whose name he selected. When asked whether wife-swapping is immoral one man answered, "It's not wrong as long as we have a meaningful relationship; furthermore, we can do what we want as long as we don't hurt anyone."

In Washington a group of protesters planted a bomb in the nation's Capitol. A few minutes after it went off, a letter was received by the Associated Press which said that the Capitol was chosen because it is the symbol of the government. The system is so corrupt, the protesters argued, that the only solution was to burn it down. If the evils of the establishment can be eliminated by demolishing banks, universities, and federal buildings, it's worth the price.

In these and countless other similar situations, the gap between traditional morality and the modern avant-garde approach is widening. The number of people who follow absolute moral principles is diminishing. This fact is used as added ammunition against traditional morality. "Everybody's doing it," is an old but popular argument. Those who predicted that there was a rumbling in the mountain of moral relativism can now proclaim that the avalanche is here. "Hardly anyone under thirty believes your view anymore," a teenager tells his parents, and he in part speaks the truth. The generation gap has become the morality gap. Insisting on personal freedom, children are urged to make their own moral decisions without accepting the values of the past.

This new emphasis on personal freedom has had some startling consequences. According to a Gallup poll taken in 1971, more than four college students out of ten have now tried marijuana. This is double the number of a year ago and eight times the number in 1967.[1] Paralleling this is the remarkable increase in the use of heroin and other hard drugs. The number of drug users is on the increase, even though medical authorities have proved that even a limited number of trips can have devastating consequences.

Statistics also indicate that major crimes have increased 284% since 1962.[2] Many people live in constant fear of being mugged, robbed, or raped. For this reason the safety of the nation's streets has become an issue in political campaigns. In addition to violent crimes, a variety of other offenses such as thefts and forgery, has skyrocketed in recent years. In 1971 a group of the nation's bankers met in Chicago to discuss the problems they share. They reported that embezzlement alone increased one hundred percent in the past year. The President's commission on law enforcement reports that in the grocery trade, the theft estimates for shoplifting and employee theft are almost equal to the total amount of profit.[3]

One of the most obvious changes in moral standards has occurred in the area of sexual freedom. Pornographic literature is sold openly, contraceptives are readily available, and books are written which describe in detail the proper procedures for having an illicit sexual affair. The movie industry has discovered that obscene films banned ten years ago are now eagerly accepted, and not even churches are complaining.

Jack Houston, in an article entitled "Profits Prove SeX-Rated Films Not A Public Gripe" stated: "Ironically, as movies have become more expressive in the exploitation of sex, agitation against their showing in neighborhood and suburban theaters has become almost nil."[4] Objections to sexual exploitation in the movie industry have become hushed, if not completely muted. Houston goes on to say that "the church, which traditionally had voiced its objection to some or all movies, depending on its particular brand of Christianity, also has become silent."[5]

Parents who have insisted on chastity are discovering that a new generation is arising which does not accept moral absolutes. A generation ago it was possible to legislate certain moral principles by stressing that morality "pays." Parents warned their children of the consequences of sexual permissiveness. But we are living in a new day. Medical science has supposedly reduced the fears that once accompanied premarital and extramarital sex, so the old arguments are no longer effective. As Pierre Burton points out in *The Comfortable Pew,* "Scientific advances have conspired to remove for many people (eventually I suggest for all people) two of the major concerns surrounding extra-marital or premarital relations: the fear of pregnancy and the fear of venereal disease."[6] He states that the deans in colleges report that traditional threats about what happens to "loose" girls no longer are effective. Then he adds, "The church, then, must be prepared to come up with other valid and logical reasons why continence should be observed outside the marriage bed."[7]

Burton may not be entirely right. The fact is that venereal disease is reaching epidemic proportions. In Los Angeles, fully one in five of the city's high school students will have contracted gonorrhea or syphilis by the time he graduates. As an infectious disease, VD is outranked in incidence only by the common cold. Furthermore, there is evidence that those who engage in sex outside of marriage find that such conduct has other undesirable consequences. A number of psychotherapists have found that the psychological effects are damaging, and many people who have sex more discover that they are enjoying it less. But Burton is not entirely wrong. With contraceptives available and proper medical remedies for venereal disease, the arguments based on fear have lost their sting. At least a large segment of the population is not buying the "you will get into trouble" package.

The same may be said of other moral issues. Moral conduct has frequently been instilled because of the penalty involved if a principle is violated. "Honesty is the best policy" is an expression that was heard a generation ago. Today it is seldom repeated for one good reason: thousands of people are realizing that it is *not* wise to be honest (at least not in financial terms). The crook generally becomes wealthy; the honest man becomes poor. Criminals are discovering that crime (unlike the fluctuating stock market) pays handsome dividends. This has caused perceptive individuals to ask, "If it doesn't pay to be honest, why bother?" *That* is an excellent question.

Since the argument from consequences no longer has retained its force, many—especially young people—who at one time intended to live within the confines of absolutes, have climbed on to the moral toboggan slide. Rather than living by fixed principles, decisions are now made situationally. Recently a coed, when deciding whether to cheat, asked an interesting philosophical question: "Which is the greater evil—

to cheat, or to flunk out of college?" For her the latter was the greater evil, so she made her decision accordingly.

Such reasoning is based on what has become known as *situation ethics.* No longer are decisions made on the basis of principle, but rather on the basis of desired results. If the old form of morality (eg., honesty, faithfulness, and continence) does not pay, perhaps it is time to have a moral theory which does. Situation ethics, by teaching that love must replace law, promises that morality can indeed pay. The value of moral actions is no longer judged in accordance with fixed rules; now only that which is loving becomes moral. In an age that cries, "Make love, not war," such an ethic may indeed appear appropriate.

However, in order for any moral viewpoint to commend itself, it must of necessity be evaluated both philosophically and theologically. If ethics is a study designed to tell people what they *ought* to do, every ethical theory must be carefully analyzed. It is hoped that this book will in a measure meet this need. The purpose of the investigation is to find the answer to three questions: Can situation ethics give guidance in making ethical choices? If so, can these choices be justified rationally? If not, is there an alternative approach which can give guidance and yet survive rational analysis?

Three further comments are necessary before the issues are fully discussed. First, no attempt is made in this book to differentiate between the new morality and situation ethics; the terms are used interchangeably. Those who insist that the new morality is limited to sexual conduct while situationism covers all aspects of morality may be partially correct. The important point is that the arguments used to determine what is moral and what is not are identical in both cases. All ethical systems which reject moral absolutes and judge conduct by its consequences or intentions have a commonness which binds them together. The playboy who justifies his relationship with a girl practices the same philosophy as the man who tells a lie to get ahead in business. The chief spokesman for situation ethics, Joseph Fletcher, has seen the point clearly. His book *Situation Ethics* properly covers a wide range of ethical issues including sexual conduct. Appropriately the subtitle of the book is *The New Morality*.

Second, *The Morality Gap* is largely an analysis of the writings of Joseph Fletcher. Mistakenly, some conclude that he is the only articulate situationist, but he is its leading proponent. Bishop John A. T. Robinson in *Honest To God* popularized this new approach to ethics, and in his own way Bishop Pike made a contribution to the situational milieu. However, Fletcher was selected because his writings provide the clearest statement of the new morality (as Bishop Robinson acknowledges), and the popularity of his book *Situation Ethics* elevated him to the position of chief spokesman for the situationists.

Although much of the debate which initially surrounded Fletcher's writings has subsided, the philosophy of situationism remains with us. Many who have never heard of Fletcher or the word *situationism* employ his *method* of making moral decisions. The clerk who weighs with his thumbs, the mechanic who needlessly replaces parts, and the secretary who dishonestly punches her time clock—these people accept the presuppositions of the new morality, even if they have not fully considered its implications. For this reason, an analysis of situationism is ever relevant.

Finally, the reader will discover that this book is not primarily concerned with specific ethical issues. The disagreement that exists as to what actions are right or wrong can only be settled by answering a more fundamental question, namely, What *makes* an action right or wrong? Whether cheating, wife-swapping or destroying public property is moral or immoral is dependent on the criteria used to judge moral actions. This book is intended to help solve this problem. Only when this question is successfully answered can specific ethical issues be evaluated with understanding.

Today a gap exists between those who believe that morality should be based on divine legislation and those who insist that man must decide for himself the difference between right and wrong. On the surface, these two views might not seem to be greatly opposed to each other; or at least it might be thought that man left by himself can arrive at some sort of a workable ethical system. Meanwhile, the gap continues to widen. But how different are these two positions? Could they ever be reconciled? Or are they so divergent that each individual must choose one or the other as the basis of his ethical philosophy?

Socrates frequently urged his companions to be patient in philosophical discussions. Sometimes when one side of an argument is presented, it sounds plausible until other arguments are considered. Since the total picture is so necessary in any discussion, the advice of Socrates is indispensable. It is hoped that the reader will follow the discussion carefully; this can only be done by reading the argument patiently to the end.

2
What Is the New Morality?

AT THE BATTLE OF THE BULGE, a Mr. Bergmeier was captured by the Russians and taken to Wales as a prisoner of war. Later his wife was picked up by a Soviet patrol and taken to a prison in the Ukraine. When Mr. Bergmeier was returned from Wales, he began looking for their children. Two of them were found in a detention school run by the Russians. The oldest, Hans, age fifteen, was found hiding in a cellar. They had no idea where their mother was but kept searching, hoping to find her.

While in prison in the Ukraine, Mrs. Bergmeier learned that her husband and family were looking for her. She longed to return to them but could only be released if she became ill or pregnant. After some contemplation, she asked a German guard to impregnate her, and he consented. A few months later she was sent back to Berlin and joined her family. They were overjoyed that she had returned, and welcomed her, even though she told them how she had managed it. When baby Deitrich was born, they loved him because he had brought the family back together. Did Mrs. Bergmeier do the right thing?

Joseph Fletcher in his book *Situation Ethics* uses this story to illustrate how the new morality is to be applied.[1] According to him there are basically three approaches in making moral decisions. All of the ethical systems of the past can be classified according to these three categories.

The first is *legalism*. Fletcher describes it as follows:

With this approach one enters into every decision-making situation encumbered with a whole apparatus of prefabricated rules and regulations. Not just the spirit but the letter of the law reigns. . . . Solutions are preset, and you can "look them up" in a book—a Bible or a confessor's manual.²

Clearly, a legalist would insist that Mrs. Bergmeier did evil when she committed adultery with the German guard. The seventh commandment, "Thou shalt not commit adultery" (Ex 20:14), would be regarded as a universal law which does not permit exception. (Whether the application of this commandment constitutes legalism will be considered later.) Traditional Christianity has regarded the precepts of the Bible as having binding authority in all situations—even when a mother is locked in a Russian prison and separated from her family. Legalists believe they know in advance whether a given act is right or wrong quite apart from the context of a given situation. The new moralists insist that such knowledge is impossible. They maintain that legalism must be rejected because it is more concerned with the law than it is with people. Rather than judging each situation individually, legalism even condemns those who break the commandments because of loving concern.

On the opposite end of the moral spectrum are the advocates of *antinomianism*. This term simply means "against law." Antinomians believe that there are no rules to follow in making ethical decisions. Each individual is thrown into a world which he cannot comprehend rationally; he is caught in a universe which gives him no principles by which he can judge moral actions. Fletcher says that the Gnostics are an example of antinomianism since their ethical decisions "are random, unpredictable, erratic, quite anomalous. Making moral decisions is a matter of spontaneity; it is literally unprincipled, purely *ad hoc* and casual."³ Contemporary existentialists are also antinomian. Sartre believes that the world cannot be comprehended rationally, therefore there can be no objective criteria for good and evil. But, he insists, an individual must decide; he cannot evade his freedom. *What* a man chooses is not important; the fact that he *does* choose is significant. The existentialists do not attempt to formulate a world view; such an ideal is regarded as impossible. The universe is basically absurd. What would the existentialists say about Mrs. Bergmeier? Presumably they would see nothing wrong with her illicit relationship. The prohibition regarding adultery would not necessarily be valid in *any* situation. Since they reject all moral principles, they have no basis to determine whether the act was moral or immoral. Furthermore, it would not really matter. The fact that she made the decision is to her credit; what she decided is a matter of indifference.

The third choice, *situationism,* better known as situation ethics or the new morality, promises to find a middle path which rejects both legalism and antinomianism.

Advocates of the new morality reject both legalism and antinomianism. Fletcher repudiates legalism because it puts principles ahead of people and emphasizes the letter of the law rather than love. Those who hastily put the new moralists into the antinomian camp have construed the new morality to be something which its adherents disavow. Antinomianism is rejected by situationists because antinomians refuse to think seriously about the demands of love. They scorn any criterion for judging a moral act.

Situationism does not reject the moral rules of the past, but neither is it bound by them. It seeks to use the rules whenever they are useful; but it discards them if they happen to conflict with *love,* which is regarded as a higher principle than law. Specifically,

> The situationist enters into every decision-making situation fully armed with the ethical maxims of his community and its heritage, and he treats them with respect as illuminators of his problems. Just the same he is prepared in any

situation to compromise them or set them aside *in the situation* if love seems better served by doing so.[4]

As a situationist, Fletcher would condone the action of Mrs. Bergmeier in the Russian prison camp. After reciting the story near the end of his book, he permits his readers to decide whether she did right or wrong; but for him the answer is obvious: she did a good and right thing. While other acts of adultery may be immoral, this one was moral because of the *situation*.

It must be emphasized that Fletcher does not merely believe that Mrs. Bergmeier committed what moral theologians frequently refer to as "the lesser of two evils." For Fletcher, such a concept has no place in morality. Mrs. Bergmeier did not do something which was both loving and wrong. If adultery, lying, or stealing is done lovingly, it is right and not the "lesser evil."

What then makes an action moral? Bishop Robinson in *Honest to God* was one of the first scholars to popularize situation ethics. For him the sole arbiter in any moral situation is love. It alone decides the morality of an act. He asserts, "If we have the heart of the matter in us, if our eye is single, then love will find the way, its own particular way in every individual situation."[5] No commandment can infringe on what love demands. Sex relations outside of marriage are not intrinsically wrong; the only intrinsic evil is lack of love.

Joseph Fletcher, whose book *Situation Ethics* is regarded by Robinson as the best articulation of the situationists' viewpoint, likewise adopts love as the only moral criterion for ethical decisions. Since he holds that love may frequently conflict with the moral laws of the Bible, he accepts only the *summary* of the law as binding. He never tires of quoting Romans 13:8: "Owe no man anything, but to love one another; for he that loveth another hath fulfilled the law." Similarly, Christ said, "Thou shalt love the Lord, thy God, with all thy heart, and with all thy soul, and with all thy mind. . . . Thou shalt love thy neighbor as thyself. On these two commandments hang all the law and the prophets" (Mt 22:37-40). For situationists this summary is the only absolute. No universal rules can be derived from the universal commandment of love. Every one of the Ten Commandments is subject to exceptions. The situationist says it is his *duty* to break any or all of them if love demands it.

Situationism therefore operates as a middle-of-the-road ethical theory. It repudiates legalism and antinomianism and asserts that "everything else without exception, all laws and rules and principles and ideals and norms, are only *contingent,* only valid *if they happen* to serve love in any situation."[6] Adultery, lying, and murder are not always wrong; in some situations they may be loving acts.

Situationism has a prima facie claim to plausibility. Traditional Christianity, with its belief in universal moral values, has often justified evil in order to avert greater evil. If love alone is the basis for moral decisions, such contradictions might be avoided. Is it not reasonable to consider the consequences of an act rather than judging the act *itself* moral or immoral? But before the relative merits of each system are evaluated— and before the question of the universal validity of the Ten Commandments be considered—the discussion must turn to a careful study of *love,* the basis of situationism.

3

The Meaning of Love

THE NEW MORALISTS choose love as their criterion for good and evil. They insist that love may frequently require that rules and commandments be set aside if the situation demands it. However, since there is widespread disagreement as to what actions are loving or unloving, a more fundamental problem must be solved; namely, what makes an action loving or unloving? Love must be defined accurately, so that a person can make an intelligent decision regarding what counts for love and what does not. As Aristotle observed, a term must not only mean something but it must mean not-something as well. There must be a limit to the meaning of a given word. Clearly, a term compatible with anything and everything is meaningless. The word *love* in particular suffers from much ambiguity because it is used in a variety of contexts. A lover may tell his girl friend, "I love you," and a moment later use the same word to describe his fondness for his mother's plum pudding or apple pie. Since agape (love) is the basis for the new morality, it might be expected that the term would be clearly defined. Unfortunately, this is not the case. Although both Joseph Fletcher and Bishop Robinson acknowledge that the word needs defining, they present a confusing and contradictory account of what love is. Several commentators have found as many as a dozen uses of the word *love* in Fletcher's book. Such a list is unnecessary. Three incompatible definitions should be sufficient to demonstrate that the new moralists must make a decision as to what description of love should be used in calculating what actions are loving and which ones fail to pass the test.

NOMINALISM

In medieval times a controversy existed between the nominalists and the realists. Fletcher acknowledges that the debate which raged for several centuries is central to the problem of ethics. The realists believed that universals had independent, objective existence, but the nominalists held that universals existed only in name (hence the word *nominalism*). Universals were regarded as nothing but collective names; only the individual things are to be regarded as substances, as the truly real. The nominalists concluded that there are no eternal moral principles which are binding in all situations. Since only the individual thing is real, morality cannot be subsumed under universal prohibitions or commandments. In making ethical choices the situation must be considered rather than invoking an absolute moral rule.

Fletcher falls squarely under the nominalist label and asserts, "The whole mind-set of the modern man, *our* mind-set, is on the nominalists' side."[1] Several scholars are then listed and subsequently judged as to whether they are consistent situationists. Brunner, Buber, Brightman, and even Barth qualify. Dietrich Bonhoeffer came close to joining the ranks, but missed it.[2] With such impressive company it seems that Fletcher can scarcely go wrong.*

In keeping with the nominalists' view that there are no fixed

---

*Fletcher labors to put as many contemporary scholars as possible in the situationist camp. Perhaps he thinks his position is more secure if it can be demonstrated that "the whole mind-set of the modern man . . . is on the nominalists' side" (p. 58). Paul Ramsey appropriately comments, "Which is enough said in behalf of mind-set even if it could be demonstrated to be a species of thoughtlessness." Paul Ramsey, *Deeds and Rules in Christian Ethics* (New York: Scribner, 1967), p. 156. For criticisms regarding Fletcher's evaluation of contemporary theologians, see pp. 154-55 of Ramsey.

moral principles, Fletcher defines love as the *intention* of the agent. He writes, "Nothing *can* justify an act except a loving purpose."[3] Love is "an attitude, a disposition . . . a purpose."[4] Moral judgments are therefore to be based on whether one's intentions were good or bad. When this criterion is used, the consequences of an act are irrelevant. If one were faced with the decision of whether to lie or tell the truth, the lie would be moral (assuming good intentions) even if it was later discovered and greater harm came as a result of it. It would be moral because it was told in love, that is, with a loving purpose.

In contrast, the realist believes that an action can have moral value independently of its consequences. Good and evil are regarded as intrinsic to the action. It follows, therefore, that an action can be immoral even if some good may happen to result from it. Also an action can be moral even if the consequences are undesirable. Traditional Christianity has adopted the realist position, because the moral law is regarded as the revealed will of God, hence obedience is required apart from a calculation of its results. This does not mean that consequences are totally unrelated to moral actions. In *a*moral matters the consequences are regarded as a factor in decisions; and even in moral issues, consequences are not regarded as irrelevant. Christianity holds that in eternity, appropriate rewards will be given for righteous deeds, and retribution for evil deeds. In that sense consequences are regarded as relevant to morality. Gordon Clark writes: "Not only will those who meet God's requirement be rewarded with joys unspeakable, but also a conscious desire for those rewards is legitimate motivation."[5] However, traditional Christianity has repudiated the basic tenets of nominalism, namely, that moral decisions are to be determined by *human* calculation.

In the twelfth century a philosopher by the name of Peter Abelard denied the existence of universal ethical norms. Like the new moralists he stressed the *individual* rather than any binding moral code. He believed that morality was dependent solely on the *intention* of the agent. Consequences cannot become the basis for moral actions. An act done with good intentions is always good; if done with evil intentions, it is always evil. Both the act per se and the results were regarded as unimportant. But at this point a crucial question arises: What basis can be used to determine whether an intention is good or evil? Have people not performed grossly immoral acts while believing that they were doing right? No one can deny that they had good intentions. Christ predicted that the day would come when those who killed His followers would do so believing that they were serving God (Jn 16:2). Abelard attempted to answer this problem by an appeal to the Scriptures. Since the Bible spells out the content of morality rather clearly (eg., the Ten Commandments and the Sermon on the Mount), one might suspect that he would be explicit in deciding which actions had right intentions and which ones did not. Though Abelard insisted that only the intention determined the morality of an act, he decided that he could not take the biblical commandments at face value. Consistent with this view he writes, "Wherever actions are restricted by some precept or prohibition, these refer rather to will and consent than to the deeds themselves."[6] The commandments may be broken without committing a sin. He held that if a person acts in ignorance, even adultery and murder may be committed without sinning. A sinner is not one who does what is prohibited, but rather he *consents* to it.

Abelard's theory that only the intention of the person determines morality led him to some rather interesting conclusions. Since no one should be judged by what he does, but by his intentions, it follows that those who disobeyed Christ (when He urged them not to make His miracles public) did the right thing. Their disobedience did not arise from contempt; therefore, it was good that they did not obey the command. Furthermore, those who persecuted Christ and ultimately killed Him should not be condemned for their deeds. In fact, Abelard says that their sin would have been greater if they would have allowed Christ and others whom they persecuted to go free.[7]

Since Fletcher has defined a moral action as one that has a loving purpose, does he accept Abelard's conclusions? The answer is yes. Fletcher writes, "Like Abelard in the twelfth century, the situationist says sturdily that those who crucified Christ according to their own consciences were guilty of no sin."[8] For Fletcher, the loving purpose alone is sufficient to make the crucifixion of Christ moral. Morality is determined by the intention of the agent.

There is, however, a second description of love which Fletcher presents. He states that "love is not something we *have* or *are,* it is something we *do.*"[9] Even more clearly he asserts, "In Christian situation ethics nothing is worth anything in and of itself. It gains or acquires its value only because it happens to help persons (thus being good) or to hurt persons (thus being bad)."[10] Here Fletcher places the basis of morality squarely on the *consequences* of an act. Throughout his writings, this meaning is stressed most often. He believes that people should manipulate circumstances and break whatever rules necessary in order to achieve certain results. Responsible individuals should be calculating and use every reasonable means available to reach desirable ends. One of the foundation stones of situationism is the pragmatism of William James and John Dewey, which holds that the good is whatever works. In fact, Fletcher states that the very first question in all ethics is *What* do I want?[11] With this as the central question, he proceeds to give a multitude of illustrations of how people in the past have gone about achieving their goals. There was a man in the English movie *The Mark* who was sexually attracted to little girls, until rescued by a woman who seduced him, thereby releasing him from his pathology.[12] In this case the woman achieved her loving goal by shrewd calculation. A Negro woman killed her crying baby with her own hands so that the Indians might not find her and her other companions. In this way their lives were spared.[13] In these and countless other illustrations, Fletcher emphasizes that moral actions are ones that are instrumental in producing certain consequences. In general, people are to be placed above principles; individuals are more important than things. But in answering the question of What do I want? the important thing is to achieve an end by using available means.

On the one hand Fletcher insists that the intention of the agent makes an act moral; while on the other hand, he maintains that an act is not moral until it helps someone. However, the two views cannot be reconciled. If an act is moral because of good intentions, then the consequences must be regarded as irrelevant. Frequently an act done with good intentions turns out to be harmful, and conversely an act done with evil intentions may by accident have good results. For example, if good intentions are the criterion for morality, then a man who has sex relations outside his marriage would not be doing evil, as long as he meant well—that is, had good intentions. If good intentions could absolve from any taint of sin those who crucified Christ, presumably this man did not sin either. At first, it might appear that his good intentions worked out perfectly. But what if, several weeks later, his wife discovers what happened, becomes enraged, sues for a divorce, and leaves with the children, who by this time have become frustrated and disillusioned with their father. In addition, the man discovers that the woman with whom he had his liaison became pregnant. Was the act moral? If morality is to be judged by his intentions, the answer is yes; if it is to be judged by consequences, the answer is no. And it is contradictory to say it is both!

Of course, such situations may also be reversed. In the Old Testament, Joseph was tempted to have an affair with Potiphar's wife. Although she coaxed him day after day, he refused. No one could doubt his good intentions; in fact, one of the reasons he resisted was his loving concern for Potiphar himself. He would not only be sinning against God, but against the one who had committed so much responsibility into his hands. Not even a situationist could quarrel with Joseph's loving intentions! Yet, because of his resistance to this woman, he was put in jail for two years. Had he been acting morally? If intentions make an act moral, then once again the answer is yes. But what if morality is judged by consequences? What if Fletcher is correct when he says, "But Christians say that nothing is right unless it *helps* somebody"?[14] To be in prison for two years when innocent is indeed an unloving consequence. Joseph, on situational grounds, would be judged immoral.

Some may argue that Joseph's imprisonment actually turned out for greater good (through circumstances he was later promoted to a high position in Egypt), and hence this act even from the standpoint of the consequences was moral. Two things must be considered: (1) it is entirely possible that Joseph would have eventually been elevated to his high position even if he had not gone to prison, and (2) the real question is What if Joseph had died in prison because of his resistance to Potiphar's wife's enticement? Doubtless, situationists would consider an innocent victim's imprisonment and death something that hurts rather than helps.

If morality is to be determined by consequences, Joseph would be regarded as immoral. What is true of Joseph would be true of all martyrs both past and present. Fletcher, when discussing a situationist's response to the second commandment, Thou shalt have no other gods before me, says "One could surely *pretend* to have no faith in God, or in any combination of gods, if it were necessary for loving cause."[15] The martyrs did not follow such advice, even when their lives and those of their families were at stake. As a result they were killed. If morality is judged by results based on this world's value system, as the situationists propose, then such conduct is immoral.

When pressed to choose between the two methods of evaluating a moral act, situationists prefer to remain ambiguous. Fletcher uses both meanings throughout his writings, giving the impression that everything is perfectly clear. There is, of course, an advantage to such double-talk; it gives the moralist an opportunity to keep shifting ground in an ethical debate. Someone like Joseph is considered moral because of his good intentions (the bad consequences are ignored); conversely an adulterer is judged by whether he hurts or helps others (consequences are the criteria for morality). Fletcher is able to jump from one corner to another, never claiming any given one as his own. Or to change the metaphor slightly, the situationist thinks he is secure in walking the middle of the road, but in reality he bumps into people going both ways. The Greeks had a race in which a man put one foot on one horse and the other foot on another horse. The race went fine as long as the horses stayed together. When they began to separate, the man had a decision to make! The situationist must also decide. He cannot have both definitions at the same time.

Fletcher has a third description of love which is quite unrelated to the two previous definitions. Love is regarded as a faculty which helps discern what to do. "Love, in the imperative mood of neighbor-concern, examining the relative facts of the situation in the indicative mood, discovers what it is obliged to do."[16] Since Fletcher rejects the idea of conscience giving direction in moral decisions, it is difficult to know how love is capable of making a moral choice. In *Honest To God* Bishop Robinson expresses a similar idea of love—that it has a built-in moral compass that intuitively relates to the need of another in a given situation.[17] Whether this definition of love is satisfactory will be discussed in subsequent chapters. It is sufficient to note here that such a view is quite distinct from the preceding accounts of what love is and how it works.

It is painfully obvious that Fletcher has not given any definition of the word *love;* he has instead presented three incompatible descriptions of how love becomes the basis for judging conduct. Each one of these three descriptions has its own peculiar difficulties; to accept all three at the same time is intolerable. It is this equivocation that led James Gustafson to remark,

> "Love," like "situation," is a word that runs through Fletcher's book like a greased pig (if I may be excused an allusion to my rural county-fair past). Nowhere does Fletcher indicate in a systematic way his various uses of it. It refers to everything he wants it to refer to.[18]

If love is the criterion for good and evil, and if there is no clear statement as to what constitutes a loving act, then morality becomes at best confusing. Some of the practical results of this theory already become evident. No one could ever be judged for an act per se; each action is morally neutral, and only the intention *or* the consequences (not both!) can be evaluated to see whether he is guilty or innocent. However, there are even more serious difficulties which accompany an ethic which is based on love without specific content. It may even be possible to demonstrate that the difficulties turn out to be impossibilities; in fact, the new morality will be shown to be neither *new* nor a system of *morality*.

UTILITARIANISM

The question of whether the new morality is really *new* is not only asked by the curious; from a philosophical standpoint, the question is of more than passing interest. Various ethical theories have been advanced since the time of Plato. Each has had its merits and shortcomings adequately exposed by friend and foe. But what of situationism? Is it a new species, or is it a revival of some previous philosophy?

The answer (to use a Barthian dialectic) is both yes and no. Since "there is nothing new under the sun," it is not surprising to find that situationism is directly related to the utilitarian theory of Jeremy Bentham and John Stuart Mill. Fletcher admits pointedly, "It takes over from Bentham and Mill the strategic principle of 'the greatest good of the greatest number.' "[19]

Bentham is generally regarded as the founder of the utilitarian movement. He discovered the principle of utility expressed by David Hume and applied it to social and ethical problems. Briefly, the theory is that moral decisions can be made by calculating the pleasures and the pains involved in the consequences of any act. In the calculation each individual is treated equally; hence morality is democratic. A moral action is one that produces more pleasure and less pain than any substitute action. In an immoral action the pain would outweigh the pleasure. But in order to achieve the correct balance, pleasures and pains must be measured. Bentham listed seven factors which are necessary to determine their value. In each calculation of pains and pleasures, one must consider the (1) intensity, (2) duration, (3) certainty or uncertainty, (4) propinquity (i.e., nearness) or remoteness, (5) fecundity (its chance of being followed by other pleasures), (6) purity (its chance of not being followed by pains), and (7) its extent (the number of people who are affected by it).[20]

Bentham then says that one must find the total degrees of good tendency (i.e., pleasure) and the total degrees of bad tendency (i.e., pain) when making a moral decision. He thought this was possible by using the seven criteria and multiplying the respective totals by the number of people involved. Morality is now on a scientific basis. Only in this way can one be sure that the greatest good for the greatest number of people will prevail—or more accurately—that the amount of pleasure in the world will be greater than the amount of pain.

Some of the practical implications of Bentham's utilitarianism are of particular interest. While it may be somewhat difficult to make moral calculations in some instances, it is apparent that the theory has frequently been implemented, especially by some political regimes. Since Bentham was interested in the principle of utility for governmental action, Gordon Clark provides a concrete example of how utilitarianism operates when properly applied. Clark writes:

> Let us suppose a nation [were] composed of ninety per cent indigenous stock, blond Nordics, and ten per cent of a despised and hated minority—Jews, for instance. Now, the indigenous, homogeneous stock, having been reared in the rigorous, warlike, and superior virtues of primitive Teutonic barbarism, finds great pleasure, not in scalping white men with tomahawks, but in a more refined and scientific torturing of Semites. It is all good, clean fun, and very profitable, too. The execution or torture of each member of the inferior race gives pleasure to millions. Even if—the point need not be debated—even if the pain of torture is greater than the pleasure of any one of the superior Nazis, the pain cannot outweigh the sum of the pleasures of the millions. If there should be any possibility of the pain's being greater than the pleasure, the least scientific of a race of scientists could easily adjust the degree of torture; or, better, the national department of education could step-up the courses in torture-appreciation. And the greatest good of the greatest number will prevail.[21]

The most famous English utilitarian was John Stuart Mill. He agreed with Bentham that the principle of utility cannot be proved; but since each person desires his own happiness, the theory was legitimate. He recognized that a fundamental problem with Bentham's hedonistic calculus was that all pleasures were considered qualitatively equal. Bentham was concerned only with the *quantity* of pleasure; Mill wanted to introduce *quality* as well into the mathematical equation. For example, he said that it was better to be Socrates *dis*satisfied than a fool satisfied. This makes the new factor of quality the moral determinant, not the pleasure as such. But if that which produces pleasure for the greatest number distinguishes a moral from an immoral act, then clearly the pleasures of sexual indulgence, guzzling liquor, playing tennis, reading Shakespeare, and those that exist on God's right hand cannot be distinguished. There is no way that we can distinguish between a high or low pleasure without merely appealing to personal preference.

Fletcher acknowledges that his ethical theory forms a coalition with Bentham and Mill. After an illustration of situationism at work he concludes, "This is the agapeic calculus. . . . Our situation ethics frankly joins forces with Mill; no rivalry here. We choose what is most 'useful' for the most people."[22] The new morality is therefore a moral system based on the utilitarianism of the past. Why then is it called the *new* morality?

One aspect of this ethical theory which is generally regarded as a novelty is that utilitarianism is given a *Christian* flavor. Thus while embracing utilitarianism, Fletcher wishes at the same time to make a slight distinction between situationism and utilitarianism. Speaking of his coalition with the theory he affirms,

> Observe that this is a genuine coalition, even though it reshapes the "good" of the utilitarians, replacing their pleasure principle with *agape*. In the coalition the hedonistic calculus becomes the agapeic calculus, the greatest amount of neighbor welfare for the largest number of neighbors possible.[23]

Thus Fletcher takes the procedural principle of utilitarianism but changes the *content* to love. In this way, he attempts to differentiate between utilitarianism and the *new* morality. The difference between the two is plausible if the *content* of love is specifically defined. Whether Fletcher—or any situationist—is capable of giving specific guidelines as to what constitutes love is a matter for dispute. Nevertheless, the new moralists attempt to do what Mill did and failed. Fletcher is evidently fully aware of the difficulty (although one would not suspect it immediately), and realizes that he is incapable of distinguishing his brand of ethics from utilitarianism. While he may insert the word *love* for pleasure, the point is that many may regard the most loving thing as that which brings pleasure while an unloving act brings pain. This throws situationism completely back into the lap of utilitarianism. Fletcher realizes that his original distinction between situationism and utilitarianism is precarious. He writes:

> We need not try to assert some supposed mutual exclusion as between *agape* and the "happiness" that utilitarians want. All depends upon what we find our happiness in: all ethics are happiness ethics. With hedonists it is one's own pleasure (physical or mental); . . . The Christian situationist's happiness is in doing God's will as it is expressed in Jesus' Summary. And his utility method sets him to seeking his happiness (pleasure, too, and self-realization!) by seeking his neighbors' good on the widest possible scale.[24]

In a more recent essay, written for professionals, Fletcher admits he has frequently avoided the issue of situationism's union with utilitarianism. He recognizes that his distinction from utilitarianism can no longer be defended. He admits the union is complete.

> But we can now cut through this issue cleanly: I am ready to turn the coalition into an organic union. Let's say plainly that *agape* is utility; love is well-being; the Christian who does not individualize or sentimentalize love *is* a utilitarian. . . . Then what remains as a difference between the Christian and most utilitarians is only the language used, and their different answers given to the question, "Why be concerned, why care?" —which is again the metaethical question.[25]

Along with utilitarianism, Fletcher is forced to accept the view that the end justifies the means. "What was once charged as an accusation against the Jesuits is here frankly embraced: *finis sanctificat media.*"[26] Fletcher relates the story of how Lenin was becoming weary of being told that he had no ethics because he used force in foreign and civil wars. Some Tolstoyan idealists accused him of believing that the end justifies the means. Finally, he shot back at them, "If the end does not justify the means, then in the name of sanity and justice, *what does?*"[27] Fletcher agrees wholeheartedly. If the end does not justify the means, then nothing else does.

Throughout history, utilitarianism with its "end justifies the means" philosophy has been implemented by political regimes. Hitler chose a certain end and had a minority group executed to achieve his desired goal. Communism has a history of bloody revolutions and massacres. All of these actions are conducted in line with the pragmatic, ethical theory of utilitarianism, with which Fletcher has formed his coalition. These leaders have spent time calculating the consequences and thereby decided what was the most useful for the most people. Morality depended on the situation.

However, situationism is not to be rejected simply because it can be used to justify torture and massacre. Consequences cannot be used to refute an ethical theory. They merely explain the practical application of the principle. If situationism is correct, the consequences will have to be accepted. While some may have a suspicion that an ethical theory which can be used to justify genocide is to be rejected, we cannot object to the theory unless it be proved that such brutality is ethically wrong. For this reason, the discussion turns to other considerations which may render the situational-utilitarian coalition untenable.

4

Love and Moral Obligation

CONSIDER a situational parable: The football stadium was jammed to capacity. Three weeks before the final game, every available ticket had been sold. There was more than the usual amount of excitement that accompanies such an event. The crowd had been warned that it was to expect a performance that varied slightly from the usual.

In previous games the teams had used the rule book; but, it was reported, the players had kept the rules only externally and without proper inward motivation. Everything was pre-fabricated. The rules were preset, and the players and officials could look them up in the manual. Sometimes there was disagreement as to whether a given player actually had violated a rule, and occasionally there were even a variety of interpretations given as to what the rule book meant; but generally the game proceeded according to a definite pattern.

For example, each team had to have the same number of players on the field, the same number of downs, and the distance gained or lost was always measured by the same standard. The players had been taught to follow the rule book ever since they started to play football. Now they (and especially the coaches) decided that it was not logical to have adult players be subject to a manual. In fact, rigid adherence to the rules had two undesirable consequences. First, the players seemed more interested in keeping the rules than in winning the game.

Often a team could have made a touchdown by breaking a single rule, but they kept the rule instead! Second, they became hypocritical in their obedience. It was a known fact that the majority of players really wanted to break the rules to win—and some would have, if they thought they could get away with it. The very presence of the rules encouraged blind obedience. However, a new day was beginning to dawn; it was a day of honesty and openness.

After some deliberation, a more contemporary scheme was devised. It was decided that the rules of football should not be considered as having *intrinsic* authority, since such a view was too legalistic for these players who had "come of age." Now each play would be judged according to the *situation*. There would be only one summary rule—*fairplay*. But since fairplay can be defined in a variety of ways, it was agreed that the term would mean "loving concern," and more specifically (lest it become an occasion for selfishness), each player should play in such a way that the greatest good (i.e., loving concern) would be distributed among the greatest number. The players were taught to be calculating, continually weighing the pros and cons; but always they were to be true to the summary rule and use any means to achieve it. There was a note of caution sounded; it was repeated several times to make certain all players got the message: The summary rule did not mean that the rules of the past were to be discarded completely! The new basis of fairplay was not antirules in any way. The rules represented the wisdom of generations of football authorities, and as such they were to be used as a bank of experience, that is, illuminators to help decide what was fairplay and what was not. Only when the rules conflicted with the summary rule of fairplay (the greatest good for the greatest number) should they be broken.

The football fans expressed various reactions to the new football regulation. A small minority insisted that utter chaos would result when it was up to each player to decide what to do on the basis of the situation. The majority, however, pointed out that the summary rule would stop the arguments that sometimes took place regarding the rule book. Often the rules seemed to conflict with the basic notion of fairplay; this led to hairsplitting and the formulation of more rules. All such contradictions would now be a thing of the past. Furthermore, the players were adults, and therefore there was no doubt that they would (1) always instinctively seek the greatest good for the greatest number, and (2) know how to act and what to do to achieve that good. Of course, no one expected one hundred percent perfection; the players might have problems guessing the results of their actions, but surely this would be an improvement over the past!

The players were interviewed before they went on the field. "Finally, I feel like a responsible individual," commented one six-foot-four quarterback. Other players had similar opinions. "It's a new age of openness and honesty," said one halfback.

The game got off to a great start. Team A had the ball and was moving progressively to team B's goal line. Then team A decided that they should call two additional players on the field because this was a home game and the majority of the fans were on their side. The summary rule indicated that anything was legitimate as long as it was for the welfare of the greatest number. Not only did the consequences permit them to break the rule, but the team was doing it with good intentions. The players were not malicious; furthermore, each believed in what he was doing. They remembered that one coach had said that good intentions alone are able to justify an act, but this team had good intentions *plus* the near certainty that the results would be in favor of the greatest number. If they did not bring in two additional players, the happiness of 50,000 fans would be at stake.

Team B was slightly disturbed. And, much to their surprise, team A learned that team B did not agree that team A's request for two more players was in keeping with fairplay.

There was some commotion (until now it had not dawned on team A that there would be any question about what constitutes fairplay), and so it was decided to stop the game and discuss the matter. Team B insisted that each of its players also had pure motives (who can argue with that); furthermore, it pointed out that while the great majority of fans present were cheering for team A, this game was being televised to team B's home city, which was nearly twice as big as team A's. Team B was deeply committed to the principle of the greatest happiness for the greatest number. If team A had two more players, team B would demand three more downs.

There was only one way this could be settled. A survey would be taken to determine the number of fans that supported each team. Then the officials could determine which team would be allowed the most players. Only in this way the happiness of the greatest number could be insured. The game was suspended for several days until the survey revealed that team B was right. In fact, the amount of happiness multiplied by the number of fans was so lopsided, that team B could have an unlimited number of players and an unlimited number of downs! This would be done out of loving concern for the greatest number.

The game was about to proceed when an unidentified fan asked, "How do you know that if team B wins the result will be the greatest good for the greatest number? The greatest good in this case is not the happiness of winning. It is the ability to be a good loser. This builds character. Anyone can accept a victory; only the truly great can be cheerful losers. Furthermore, winners of such an important game usually succumb to debauchery during their drunken celebrations. If team B would be content with a few players and they lost, then the team would win the greatest honor of all—bravery. And their fans would identify with such a victory."

The officials recognized that this new view of fairplay would ruin their previous calculations. They generally disagreed with this outspoken fan, but what really irritated them most was that they could not prove him wrong. They were forced to admit their view of what constituted the greatest good for the greatest number was a personal judgment and it was difficult, if not impossible, to determine who was right. They decided, however, that before they made their next survey, they had to be clearer as to what the greatest good really is and find some way to defend it.

* * *

The new morality is built on the premise that *love* alone is able to give guidance in making moral decisions. No serious-minded person would suggest that a game of football could be played without rules, but the situationist is willing to play the game of life without them. Fletcher states, "For the situation-ist there are no rules—none at all."[1] The question arises: Is the summary rule of love able to give more guidance in life than the summary rule of fairplay in football? Or are both of them equally meaningless in making decisions?

It has been noted that situation ethics embraces the theory that the end justifies the means. Love, when applied will al-ways seek a desired end and then find a means to achieve it. The question that must be settled is Can love establish a valid goal so that actions can be judged on the basis of whether the goal is reached? In short, is love per se capable of telling us what ends are loving and which ones are unloving?

Behind these questions lies the philosophical problem of axiology. What should be regarded as valuable? Fletcher ad-mits that the most fundamental issue in ethics is value.[2] For him, the greatest value is love; but this puts the matter back where it began; namely, what counts for love? By what scale should values be judged? Virtually every human being makes decisions from day to day on the basis of his own value system. Some consider money of greater value than education, others consider pleasure of more worth than rearing children; some prefer prestige to sexual purity; some consider communism of more value than Christianity; and others prefer drunkenness to sobriety. The decisions made by various individuals are then in harmony with their preestablished values. If one considers money of greater value than education, he will make decisions to reach the goal of money, even if it means bypassing a good education. All such decisions are made on the basis of what is regarded as valuable and what is not.

The situationist makes his moral decisions in the same way. If morality is judged by the consequences, it is necessary to decide beforehand what consequences are valuable and then act accordingly. The new moralist determines what is loving on the basis of his personal system of values. Therefore, the decisions are not based on *love* per se—such decisions are impossible! Fletcher comes to every decision fully armed with his private value judgments and gives his verdict accordingly. As Lawrence Richards puts it:

> Fletcher's decision is reached by the judgment that release from unjust exploitation by adultery is preferable to continued exploitation with chastity; that abortion is preferable to risking possible ill effects on the unwed mother. Once these value judgments have been made, love can demand the appropriate decision. *But it was not on the basis of "love" that the initial judgments were made!* The judging and weighing of the factors in the situation were—*and must logically have been*—prior to the application of the principle of love.[3]

This accounts for the fact that Fletcher's ethical views are judged according to his preconceived value system. Love is not even permitted to make a judgment in a specific situation. Consider the legalistic dictum, *"No unwanted and unintended baby should ever be born."*[4] Fletcher makes this judgment apart from a specific case (whether the pregnant woman is married or single, regardless of the stage of the pregnancy, or whether the father wants the child), and thus proves that decisions are really not made by love in the *situation*.

Richards again declares:

> What actually happens is that the situationist establishes his facts, applies values *other than love* to sort them and weigh the possible ends-in-view, and *then* drags in love and misrepresents it as the principle justifying the choice which he has already made.[5]

The dilemma of the new morality can be demonstrated by using a number of illustrations which show that the ends chosen are arbitrary and personal. Furthermore, so many different value systems are tolerated under the situational umbrella that the notion is useless as a method of ethical decision. The conclusions of the two following stories could have been reversed without any surprise to the reader. The first concerns officer Holmes who ordered most of the males aboard his ship to be thrown into the sea lest the overcrowded lifeboat founder and all lives be lost. Fletcher's criticism in this case is directed at the judge who had Holmes convicted of murder. Situation ethics says Holmes did a good thing.[6]

On the same page is the story of Capt. Scott who, when leading an expedition to the South Pole, discovered that one of his men was injured and had to be carried. Without the injured man they all would have made it to the coast. But Scott decided that he and his men would stay with the man, and thus they all perished. Incredible though it may be, Fletcher says it was a good decision! This is a complete contradiction of Fletcher's remark that more neighbors must be served rather than fewer.[7] A consistent application of the principle would have meant that Scott should have abandoned the injured man, and thereby saved his life and the lives of the other men. Speaking of these two cases, Ramsey comments:

> Yet I seriously suggest that Fletcher's notations could be reversed in these two cases with no more puzzlement to the reader. Holmes might have been honored for perishing with all the lives aboard since not all could be saved, . . . and Cap-

tain Scott might have been praised for doing the brave, good deed of getting his party safely to the coast in the only way this could possibly be done (by abandoning the injured man).[8]

The point in these illustrations is not to agree or disagree with the ethical decisions made. These cases simply illustrate that as Fletcher moves from case to case, the conclusions reached could have been reversed. The fact that Fletcher's decisions are unpredictable and contradictory shows that love alone cannot give specific guidance in making moral choices.

There are, however, other illustrations which Fletcher gives that provide a more serious threat to situationism. In fact, the threat may turn out to be a deathblow. It has already been demonstrated that Hitler attempted genocide to achieve what he believed were worthy ends. He, like every situationist, had established his value system and acted accordingly. Perhaps advocates of the new morality resent this association with Der Führer, since he is generally credited with a doubtful reputation. Fletcher would have consented to have him assassinated. But can situationists logically condemn him? Can it be proved that his value system was wrong?

Fletcher admits that situation ethics is not limited to Christians. Others with divergent value systems qualify as well; they are all doing what they consider to be most loving. He concedes,

> The Christian situationist says to the non-Christian situationist who is also neighbor—or person—concerned: *"Your* love is like mine, like everybody's; it is the Holy Spirit. . . . God *is* love, he doesn't merely *have* it or *give* it; he gives himself—to all men, to all sorts and conditions: to believers and unbelievers, high and low, dark and pale, learned and ignorant, Marxists and Christians and Hottentots."[9]

Since the love Fletcher speaks about is available to all, he recognizes that situationism can include virtually anyone. Even atheists qualify. His willingness to acknowledge this is further proof that the ends which determine the validity of moral acts are completely undefined. He declares,

> An atheist could be a situationist, or an egoist, or a vitalist —anybody who, no matter what his formal imperative may be (love, self-interest, life, or whatever), cuts his coat to fit each situation. Lots of atheists, for example, make love their imperative, and often they outdo Christians in their faithful service to it—even if their reason (motive) is neither Christological or theological.[10]

Since Fletcher believes God gives His love to Marxists and atheists as well, they rightly fall under the situationist label. Fletcher says that a Viet Cong terrorist who walks into a Saigon officers' mess and pulls the pin in a bomb hidden under his coat is an example of an altruistic ethic; and other illustrations like it are examples of selfless concern for others.[11] Of course, the Viet Cong terrorist did the most loving thing—given his system of values.

One more example will be taken from Fletcher's writings before summarizing the issue being considered. During World War II, a priest bombed a Nazi freight train. In response, the Nazis began to kill twenty hostages a day until the guilty person surrendered. Three days later a Communist (a fellow resistance fighter) betrayed the priest. When asked why he refused to give himself up, the priest said, "There is no other priest available and our people's souls need my absolution for their eternal salvation."[12] Having read this far, one would expect Fletcher to say that the priest was not doing the most loving thing. But Fletcher (startling though it may be) says, "One may accept the priest's assumptions about salvation or not (the Communist evidently did not), but no situationist could quarrel with his *method* of ethical analysis and decision."[13] Given the priest's set of values, he was doing the most loving thing.* But the Communist also thought *he* was doing the most loving thing in stopping the daily massacre. Because they could not agree on a system of values, they did not agree on an ethical decision. This illustration shows with horrifying clarity the problem of situationism. With what scale should these relative values be weighed?

In the illustration above, Fletcher introduced a new element which cannot be overlooked. The priest in the story refused to give himself up because of his belief in some spiritual consequences rather than those based merely on human calculation. If spiritual values are introduced into the vast agapeic calculus, then indeed not only Catholicism, but New Testament Christianity is also a situational ethic. What if one were to place great value on *eternal* consequences? The apostle Paul indicated that he was willing to endure hardships and be obedient because of his value system. Because he believed that God controls all consequences, he felt that the most loving thing was obedience to God. Regarding eternal values he writes:

> For our light affliction, which is but for a moment, worketh for us a far more exceeding and eternal weight of glory, While we look not at the things which are seen, but at the things which are not seen; for the things which are seen are temporal, but the things which are not seen are eternal (2 Co 4:17-18).

If Fletcher holds that the priest was acting situationally because he did the most loving thing in accordance with his religious values, then the apostle Paul would also qualify as a situationist. He lived his life in accordance with his value system, and tradition says he was martyred for it. Since he be-

---

*Since Fletcher here allows spiritual values to be also considered in the calculus, some of his previous statements are perplexing. In discussing the first commandment he says, "One could surely *pretend* to have no faith in God, or in any combination of gods, if it were necessary for a loving cause" (p. 72). But if one actually believed in a personal God, he might feel that the most loving thing is not to be a hypocrite, since God may bring about drastic results for breaking one of His commandments. The calculation of eternal consequences constitutes a good argument for the view that morality cannot be judged by human calculation.

lieved that God will condemn forever those who reject Christ, Paul spent his life doing the most loving thing, namely, preaching the gospel and urging men to be reconciled to God. He was not particularly interested in social reform or getting out of a Roman prison. He valued God's eternal rewards so highly that he was obedient to God's commands (Ac 26:19). All Christians agree with Paul that it is important to do the most loving thing, and for them it is doing the will of God, since He controls the consequences.

Fletcher might also have given other illustrations of biblical characters who were willing to die for principles of righteousness. Daniel, Jeremiah, and John the Baptist, along with scores of Christians both past and present, would serve as beautiful illustrations of those who never lie, cheat, or commit adultery to get out of a prison camp. Their motivation was their value system. They believed "that the sufferings of this present time are not worthy to be compared with the glory which shall be revealed in us" (Ro 8:18). Then, Fletcher *might* have said, "One may or may not accept their view of eternity, but no situationist can quarrel with their method of ethical analysis and decision."

In this sense, Christ also was a situationist when He went to the cross. (That His value system differed radically from Fletcher's will be seen in chapter 8.) Clearly, He did not follow Fletcher's suggestions on how to be a hypocrite to avoid undesirable earthly consequences by only *pretending* He had devotion to God the Father.[14] But Christ *was* a situationist. "The Son of man came, not to be ministered unto but to minister, and to give his life a ransom for many" (Mk 10:45). He calculated the eternal consequences of fulfilling the commandment of God the Father. Moses also was a situationist, but his value system was quite unlike Fletcher's, as can be seen from the biblical record.

By faith Moses, when he was come to years, refused to be

called the son of Pharaoh's daughter, choosing rather to suffer
affliction with the people of God than to enjoy the pleasures of
sin for a season, Esteeming the reproach of Christ greater
riches than the treasures in Egypt; for he had respect unto the
recompence of the reward (Heb 11:24-26).

Moses believed that the most loving thing was to turn from
earthly riches and to follow God. Lenin also was a situationist
who believed that a classless society was of more value than
the lives of the people massacred to bring it about.† And so
were the leaders of the Inquisition who believed that the eternal
salvation of a few was of more value than the physical lives of
the heretics. And so is the Hindu woman who throws the best
of her two babies into the Ganges River because she believes
the gods will reward her and her family by providing food and
keeping evil spirits away.

A Communist, Catholic, Puritan, Christian, Protestant, and
Hindu can all be situationists. They are all doing the most
loving thing in harmony with their system of values. The
crucial question is Whose values are right? Fletcher naïvely
assumes that everyone will agree on what is loving. Nothing
could be farther from the truth. Basil Mitchell has carefully
observed:

> There is a pervasive assumption throughout Fletcher's
> book that the "facts of the case" in themselves are always
> unproblematic and that there will, among reasonable men, be
> no difficulty in determining what will help or harm people,
> what is fair or unfair to them. The truth is, surely, that in
> many fields these are matters of deep controversy to which
> people's attitudes are influenced by their religious and meta-
> physical beliefs; so that there is little prospect of discussing
> moral questions fruitfully without a careful and sympathetic

†It is of interest that Fletcher uses Lenin as an example of one who saw clearly
that the end justifies the means (p. 121). Situationally, communism is free to
choose any end it wishes and use the appropriate means to achieve its goals. This
accounts for the massacre, brutality, and suppression exercised in communist countries.

endeavor to understand the different forms of thought in terms of which they are interpreted.[15]

Fletcher cannot escape the fact that he has provided no solutions as to what ends are to be sought. His book *Moral Responsibility* was written to discuss the practical application of his system. Apart from his private moral judgments (some have already been referred to; others will yet be considered), no attempt is made to provide coherent reasons for his value judgments. It is evident that love cut loose from any specific value system cannot give guidance in making ethical decisions. To tell individuals to do that which is "most loving" is utterly useless. Each person comes to a situation with his own value system and does what he thinks is loving, that is, right. Morality has been reduced to a matter of personal preference.

In the book of Judges, the writer describes the chaos in these words, "In those days there was no king in Israel; every man did that which was right in his own eyes" (Judg 21:25). Note that the record does not say that each did *wrong,* rather that every man did what was *right*—in accordance with his value system. The new morality tells us to do right, but it is up to each individual to decide what that means. It does no good to protest that "people are put ahead of principles," or "individuals are to be *loved*; only *things* are to be used." People, things, and principles are so closely interfused that they cannot be sorted out.

In one American city, a plot of land was cleared away for a new department store. Some of the residents staged a demonstration protesting that the new structure would ruin the beautiful scenery in the area. One indignant female protester (perhaps a briefed situationist) said, "That's the trouble with all of you; you are concerned only about things, not people." Yet if someone would have, at that moment, snatched her purse, she would likely have become angry! The reply to her could simply be, "That's the trouble with you! You are only concerned about things, not people!"

If ethics is a normative study that should tell people what they *ought* to do, the new morality is a tragic failure. As Ramsey puts it, "Where everything may count for loving, then nothing can significantly count for loving."[16] The only difference between the rule of *fairplay* in the game of football and *love* in the game of life is that football is usually played for fun; life, however, is played for keeps. Too much is at stake in moral matters to simply say, "Do the most loving thing!" Some people might take it seriously, and the parable of the football game will turn out to be the nightmare of real life.

5

Love and Predicting Consequences

IN THE STATEMENT "The end justifies the means," there are two factors, namely, the end and the means. It has already been demonstrated that situationism (which adopts this philosophy) is unable to give direction as to what ends are desirable, that is, loving. In fact, there is no agreement whatever as to what ends love is to seek. Yet, there is a further criticism of situationism.

Let us assume that a detailed value system could be provided. Suppose that all of the theological and philosophical debates of the past were finally settled, and Fletcher would be able to provide a detailed account of what ends are valuable. Situationism still could not give moral direction because it is impossible to predict the consequences of action. In other words, one could never be sure if the *means* employed would achieve the desired *ends*.

Fletcher candidly admits, "We can't always guess the future, even though we are always being forced to try."[1] Yet the fact is that unless certain desired consequences result, the action is then immoral. Fletcher must be taken at face value when he says (despite the contradiction that motives determine morality), "Christians say that nothing is right unless it *helps* somebody."[2]

G. E. Moore in *Principia Ethica* gives a lucid account of the difficulties in predicting moral consequences. He reminds us

51

that it is not sufficient to calculate only the immediate results, rather we must take account of all consequences throughout an infinite future. The chain reaction set in motion by an act would have to be calculated in toto. This means that we would need some reason to believe that no consequence of our action in the future will reverse the balance of good which we hope will be accomplished by our act. Clearly, such prognostication demands omniscience. Moore correctly writes, "Our utter ignorance of the far future gives us no justification for saying that it is even probably right to choose the greater good within the region over which a probable forecast may extend."[3]

After summarizing the problem distinctly, Moore attempts to answer his own objection by suggesting that after a few centuries the effects of an action would only be trifling; the immediate consequences are more prominent, and therefore, we can assume that the distant future need not enter into the calculation. But such an assumption is unprovable. Therefore, he adds, "Failing such a proof, we can certainly have no rational ground for asserting that one of two alternatives is even probably right and another wrong."[4]

The fact is that it is impossible to predict even the most immediate consequences of any action. If we judge morality by results, as a minimum we must know (1) all immediate consequences and the number of people affected, (2) the remote consequences and the number of people involved, and (3) the length of time each result (good or bad) lasted in each case. Thus the number of people could be multiplied by the length of desirable or undesirable consequences to determine which decision is moral.

Throughout Fletcher's books it is assumed that the consequences are always certain, but usually the relative details of the consequences are not even considered. Fletcher attempts to avoid this criticism of situationism by ignoring the matter or pretending it does not exist. He modestly admits that there is human error and that situationism may assume too much when it holds that people have the ability to know the facts and weigh them. Yet for the most part, Fletcher assumes that consequences can be easily predicted and tabulated. Only such naïveté can account for his doctrinaire ethical judgments.

Two illustrations will be given to show how imprecisely consequences are calculated. A Puerto Rican woman in East Harlem made friends with a married man in order to have a child. When the minister told her she should repent, she replied, "Repent? I ain't repentin'. I asked the Lord for my boy. He's a gift from God." Fletcher's verdict is: "She is *right.*"[5] His judgment does not merely refer to the goodness of the gift of the son. Fletcher believes she was right in the *act done.* He gives us no clue as to how his verdict was so confidently reached. There is no evidence that all of the consequences were accurately calculated.

In this case the man enticed was married. What was the outcome of this liaison so far as his wife was concerned? Did it help their marriage? Did it ruin it? Did they have children? If so, what effect did the unfaithfulness of their father have on them? What about the spiritual and psychological effect on the man who broke his marriage vows? These are only a few of the questions which would have to be accurately calculated before Fletcher could say the woman did right. Apparently, his verdict was reached completely apart from the facts of the situation. No attempt is made to calculate all of the relevant factors. Upon discussing the consequences of acquiring such a simple object as a thesaurus, he writes:

> Finally, every serious decision maker needs to ask the fourth question, What are the foreseeable *consequences?* Given any course of action, in the context of the problem, what are the effects directly and indirectly brought about, the immediate consequences, and the remote (sequelae)? This last question means, we must note, that there are more results entailed than just the end wanted, and they *all* have to be weighed and weighted. Along with getting the thesaurus,

there may come other things: impoverishment, a neurosis nurtured, professional growth, resentment by a wife or creditor, successful completion of an important thesis.[6]

Yet in the instance of the illegitimate child (involving consequences much more complicated than those of acquiring a thesaurus), Fletcher did not carefully weigh the results even *after* the action happened. It is obvious that to calculate the consequences *before* making a moral decision is even more difficult.

When discussing his view regarding the identity of love and justice, he repeats a story about an Indian who was deeply in debt; he inherited a fortune and gave it away to the poor, leaving his creditors unpaid. This story has been used at times to show that love and justice sometimes are at variance. Fletcher believes love and justice are the same. Inexplicably, he says, "The Indian failed in *agape,* and was therefore unjust."[7] Once again (since Fletcher quotes the story from another source), he made his verdict without a calculation of the facts in the situation. From a situational standpoint, the Indian should be commended for doing the right thing. Is it not "probable" that the poor needed the money more than the creditors? Surely by helping the poor the Indian was doing what he considered to be the greatest good for the greatest number. He was concerned about serving more neighbors rather than fewer, as Fletcher suggests we do. Situationally, the only way the Indian could be condemned is if Fletcher could prove that the good done to the poor was less than the harm done to the creditors. At any rate no judgment can be made upon the Indian unless all of the facts are considered.

The impossibility of such ethical calculations can be demonstrated by reading Bentham, who attempted to make moral decisions on the basis of mathematical calculations. Even the simplest ethical decision is impossible on such a basis. Suppose one is faced with the ethical decision of telling a lie to an employer. If he tells the truth, he suspects (who can know for sure!) he will be fired. If he is fired, what will the consequences be? He may find a better job and make more money, or he may find one that pays less. Can he predict how far he will be able to work his way up in each case? Perhaps he will be better off in the long run if he is fired. But what if he tells a lie and is not fired? Other questions must also be answered. If his lie is detected, will his fellow employees find out? How will they react? How will all of the related factors balance out over an extended period?

Of course, Fletcher would answer by saying that probability is sufficient. But Clark, when speaking about a similar situation asks,

> How can the required knowledge of what is probable be obtained? . . . It would require the original calculation to be completed in a large number of situations; and only when these results can be tabulated, could it be seen whether or not lying is usually unprofitable.[8]

An actual instance of lying will serve to illustrate how untenable situationism is in practice. Several years ago the State Department lied about the U-2 spy plane incident. This may have been done out of love for 180 million Americans, because their trust in the honesty of the government is crucial. Also it preserved good relations with Russia and kept a military secret which was necessary to insure future security measures. Although the original explanation by the State Department was plausible, the lie was discovered. This resulted in greater hatred among nations, and the confidence of many Americans was lost. Was the lie the *right* thing to do in that situation?

It is difficult to know how Fletcher would answer, but if an action is not right unless it helps somebody, then, the lie was moral only until it was discovered. Afterward it resulted in greater harm for the greatest number. Despite the initial embarrassment, goodwill would have been gained by the nations of the world if the truth had immediately been told. If Fletcher were to say that the lie was moral because of the good intentions, he would again be contradicting his basic thesis that only what helps people is good. (Even legalists have good intentions!) Also, he would be falling into the very error he elsewhere deplores. To assert that a lie is moral merely because of good motives (apart from good consequences) is to have an *intrinsic* view of right and wrong; namely, the lie is inherently right regardless of the outcome. If this is what Fletcher believes, he cannot criticize legalists who insist that a lie is always *evil* apart from its outcome!

Logically, we might assume that a situationist would hold that the lie (though told lovingly) was immoral. If this is the case, the fact that results cannot be predicted is highlighted. Even probability is so remote that no individual can make an ethical judgment with certainty. In fact, no decision could be classified as moral until all of the results were tabulated and weighed mathematically. On a practical level, morality is impossible.

But even if the results could be computed, the calculations would still not be complete. For in addition to the results, the motives of action (despite the contradiction noted) would also have to be evaluated. "The new morality weighs motive heavily [*sic*] in its scales, along with means and ends."[9] Exactly what Fletcher means by "heavily" is undetermined. The *intensity* of the motive would also have to be calculated in order for it to be weighed. Add to this the question of what motives are desirable, and morality becomes out of reach.

Fletcher apparently is not concerned with calculations. He does acknowledge that "with the development of computers all sorts of analytical ethical possibilities open up."[10] However, computers would not only have to be able to predict the future (so far little success has come from such attempts), but also some decisions would have to be made as to what kind of a future should be sought. Fletcher theorizes: "It is possible that by learning how to assign numerical values to the factors at stake in problems of conscience, love's calculations can gain accuracy in an ethical *ars major*."[11] However, such calculations are as yet impossible. In the meantime no person can ever be sure he is making a moral decision. Hence, the moral life is as yet impossible too.

Fletcher often ridicules legalists, asserting that they "like to wallow or cower in the security of the law."[12] While such colorful ad hominem arguments seem to put the "intrinsicalists" on the side of ignorance and insecurity, Fletcher has not provided an alternative that can survive analysis. Until he does so, he is in no position to criticize those who believe that morality should be within the ability of the humble and uneducated. With Fletcher's view, only the educated who are capable of shrewd manipulation and scientific calculation have the possibility of being moral. Perhaps morality is not beyond the reach of the common man. This can only be true, however, if the moral worth of an action is sought in the act itself and not in its results.

6

Love and the Extrinsic Fallacy

PICTURE A MAN sitting on the end of a horizontal steel bar. He is kept in balance by the weight of another man sitting on the opposite end. The bar itself is suspended from a rope fastened over the edge of a cliff. One man steadies himself enough to pull a gun from his vest pocket. He aims carefully and shoots the man at the other end. The obvious result: both men fall into the chasm below. When situationists attempt to destroy the intrinsic value of right and wrong, can they do so without destroying themselves?

It has already been noted that situationism does not accept any types of moral actions as having inherent value. Actions such as lying, cheating, killing, adultery, and cannibalism are ethically neutral—only the situation *makes* them good or evil. It follows then, that the concept of the "lesser of two evils" has no part in the situationist's philosophy. Speaking to the point, Fletcher writes:

> The idea of "greater good" makes sense, but the concept of "the lesser evil" in its ordinary form has no place in a situational ethic. It recognizes no intrinsic evil except ill will or "malice" and no intrinsic good except good will or love.[1]

It is this philosophy that forms the basis of situation ethics. If there were absolutes (intrinsic values), then actions would not be made right or wrong merely by the situation. Fletcher does not teach that certain actions are always wrong but that under certain conditions they may be done because of expediency. All actions are regarded by him as morally neutral; the situation makes them right or wrong.

Fletcher uses an illustration to differentiate between legalism and situationism which betrays his complete misunderstanding of the issues. Quoting a situationist, he compares moral rules to such rules of thumb as "punt on the fourth down" in football, or "second hand low" in the game of bridge.[2] What Fletcher evidently does not comprehend is that these rules are not rules of the game; these are only rules of practice which can be discarded if the situation calls for it. They are maxims which give guidance *within* the rules of the game. Punting on the fourth down in football is just as legal as deciding not to punt. In either case no rule has been violated. However, a football team cannot decide to have the ball for five downs or to have additional players on the field. In fact, no game can be played without some rules, even if they are kept legalistically! It follows that if there are no rules, no action can be considered better than another. Where there are no rules, there can be no transgression. Virtually no action can be considered wrong unless a rule is invoked. As was stated earlier, no conduct can be considered wrong on a football field apart from rules. To use a summary rule, "fairplay" would be of no value in determining right or wrong. For such distinctions, rules must be used as a standard.

Fletcher, however, is willing to play the game of life without rules. He holds that there are no rules that must be followed. This is consistent with his view that there are no intrinsic values. If rules do exist, the "extrinsic" view of situationism is false. Occasionally, Fletcher contradicts his basic system and in so doing destroys his extrinsic position. An example is his statement "*No unwanted and unintended* baby should ever [*sic*] be born."[3] It is not enough simply to see this statement as a direct contradiction of his official position: "The situationist avoids words like 'never' and 'perfect' and 'always' and 'complete' as he avoids the plague, as he avoids 'absolutely.' "[4] Perhaps every author should be permitted at least a few contradictions. But the issue is much more serious. The remark regarding unwanted and unintended babies is one of the few statements in Fletcher's books which give specific direction for ethical decisions. But in giving this rule, Fletcher has had to leave the extrinsic camp and join the legalists who believe in universal laws!

Another example is even more remarkable. When speaking about the possibility of being confused about what to do in matters of sexual conduct, Fletcher makes the incredible remark, "What counts is being honest. In some cases, decision can be mistaken. Let honesty reign then too."[5] Such a remark coming from a situationist is indeed strange—and contradictory.

Fletcher repeatedly has given his complete approval to dishonesty. How can he suddenly speak of honesty as though it has intrinsic value? Dishonesty is one of the situationist's most important tools, and Fletcher encourages it in every conceivable form. If harm has been done in a sexual relationship, dishonesty is just as moral as honesty; there is no reason for honesty to reign. Fletcher's unguarded lapse into the intrinsic position causes him to make a remark which again gives guidance in making ethical choices. If honesty reigns, then many decisions become very easy to judge morally. But whenever situationism provides so much as one rule for ethical conduct ("let honesty reign"), it contradicts its basic presupposition, that values are extrinsic and not intrinsic to the moral act. Fletcher is aware of this. He writes: "The insistent demand to spell out the 'content of love' masks an insistence on norms as prefabricated decisions. To 'fill up' love with rules or laws is to slip back into a new form of legalism."[6]

Up to this point in the book it has been assumed that if situationism could determine what ends are valuable and provide a basis for predicting consequences, it could be a plausible ethical theory. But now it can be seen that if situationism *were* able to provide answers for these questions (so far it has not), the theory would destroy itself. To answer the questions would be to contradict its basic presuppositions. Like the man balancing on one end of the steel bar, Fletcher's attack on intrinsic morality turns out to be an attack against himself.

A question was raised earlier in this book: What ends should be counted as loving? This can never be answered by Fletcher; if it were answered, situationism would be demolished. And since no rules can be given for loving actions, one type of conduct cannot be recommended above another. Fletcher cannot say, for example, that cannibalism is wrong. To say this is to speak of inherent evil apart from the situation. If it be argued that cannibalism *always* hurts people, it need only be remembered that hurting is often necessary when the greatest good for the greatest number is at stake. Since the end justifies the means the end need only be loving (even the immediate end need not be loving since one end can become the means to another end, which in turn becomes the means to another, etc.). A system of ethics which cannot *rule* out (there is that word again!) any type of moral action, must be equally tolerant of Puritanism and cannibalism. It cannot even say no one should ever be legalistic!

In concluding this chapter, one more observation is in order. Fletcher has repeatedly stated that love is the highest good. He should be granted the privilege of choosing his basic presupposition and building his theory upon it. If Fletcher had chosen love as his summum bonum and then spelled out specific ends and means to achieve love, he would have ended with the intrinsicalist position, but at least his ethical system would then have given moral direction. However, Fletcher selected love as his absolute, and then combined it with the pragmatism of William James and John Dewey, both of whom believed that there was no ultimate or intrinsic good. In keeping with their view, Fletcher says, "All are agreed: the good is what works, what is expedient, what gives satisfaction."[7]

Linked with pragmatism is relativism, which Fletcher also embraces. He attempts to escape the consequences of relativism by establishing one fixed absolute—*love.* Thus, all things are relative, but only relative in relationship to a fixed absolute. But is this consistent? Is it possible to embrace relativism and still cling to one absolute? Or does not the existence of one absolute disprove the pragmatic, relative view? If truth is what works, may not the day come when love will not work anymore? Perhaps that day is already here.

The conflict that exists between holding an absolute and a relative theory is clearly apparent in Fletcher's writings. He acknowledges:

> But it is of special importance here to emphasize from the situationist's angle of vision, that *ends,* like means, are relative, that all ends and means are related to each other in a contributory hierarchy, and that *in their turn* all ends become means to some end higher than themselves.[8]

This is a summary exposition of the pragmatic-relativistic philosophy. Both ends and means are relative. What is good today may not be good tomorrow. In the next sentence of the same paragraph, Fletcher resorts to his absolute. He says, "There is only one end, one goal, one purpose which is not relative and contingent, always an end in itself. Love."[9] But what shall we make of the previous statement that ends also are relative? And since all ends become means to higher ends, how can Fletcher be sure that love will always be the ultimate end? May not love be a means to another end, which in turn is a means to another—ad infinitum? Dewey would say so. But, if Fletcher's relativism is true, why might not love itself already be an obsolete end? In fact, the day might come when every value judgment made by Fletcher could be reversed. Moralists may begin to value principles more than people; hate may be substituted for love, and legalism might replace situationism. Could Fletcher give a reasoned argument against such a change? The answer must be no. Remember, both ends and means are relative. What is good today may be evil tomorrow.

Like the spider who tried to build her web on the moving hands of a clock, Fletcher attempts to establish a solid anchor with an ethical theory which *by definition* cannot have any unchangeable absolute. As has been stated, Fletcher may be granted his basic value, but when he combines this absolute with relativism, his system has a serious contradiction. Logically, if situationism (based on relativism) is true, then it is false (love no longer remains as the ultimate end).

Fletcher has stated:

> Even today, in spite of a revival of Biblical theology, three difficulties about an agapeic ethic remain: (1) People do not understand the concept itself; (2) it is resisted philosophically and ethically even when it *is* understood; and (3) it is not central in Christian church teaching despite its centrality in the New Testament.[10]

The third of these statements is questionable (it will be discussed in chapter 8). But in addition to these three reasons, three other "difficulties" about the Fletcherian agapeic ethic may now be listed: (1) it can give no guidance whatever in making moral decisions, (2) its failure to predict consequences makes morality beyond reach, and (3) it is self-contradictory. If it is true, it is false.

7

The Love Ethic Applied

IN THE MINDS of many, the new morality is generally associated with the so-called sexual revolution which is taking place today. While sexuality is only one part of the total spectrum of moral conduct, it is in this area that the new morality has had its greatest impact. With hard core pornography available everywhere and paperbacks that cover every conceivable form of sexual perversion, young people find the moral pressures too difficult to endure. More recently dormitories in many universities are coeducational; sexual partners are readily available, and the majority are not bypassing opportunities.

One of the most popular advocates of sexual permissiveness is Hugh Hefner, whose *Playboy* magazine has a paid circulation of five million. He recommends casual sex to be enjoyed by all —married or unmarried. Not all new moralists would agree with Hefner's philosophy of sex, but in general they would agree that sex is not to be limited to married partners. Fletcher welcomes the modern approach which does not condemn sex outside of marriage. When speaking of having sex relations outside of marriage, he says it is not wrong unless the partners hurt themselves or others. Then he adds, "All situationists would agree with Mrs. Patrick Campbell's remark that they can do what they want 'as long as they don't do it in the street and frighten the horses.' "[1] What determines whether sex is moral? The answer is the same as for other ethical decisions—

love. Fletcher defends Hugh Hefner from those who would accuse the *Playboy* philosophy of using girls as impersonal instruments for self-gratification. Speaking of Hefner he says, "Even though he denies that mutual commitment needs to go the radical lengths of marriage, he sees at least the difference between casual sex and straight callous congress."[2] Thus sexual acts outside of marriage are considered moral if they have the elements of caring, concern, and—above all—*love.*

There is a popular variation of this viewpoint that frequently is heard. An actress who played the part of a sex goddess in a recent movie was asked how she could perform sexual acts publicly on film. Her answer was, "I never thought I'd be able to—but I just believed so much in what we were doing—that made the difference." The fifteen-year-old girl who played the part of a foul-mouthed prostitute in the play *The Owl and the Pussycat* answered her conservative critics with the remark, "Though I didn't like the language, I felt that the play had something very important to say."[3]

These examples show that much sexual permissiveness is condoned because of *motives.* If a person says, "We did it in love"; or, "I believed in what I was doing"; somehow, it is believed the act becomes moral—but does it? It has already been argued that motives cannot be regarded as the sole criterion for morality. Such an ethical philosophy is possible only if the content of good and bad motives is spelled out in detail. If this is not done, virtually *all* conduct (including legalism) would have to be condoned without rebuke; the cannibal who believes in what he is doing and acts situationally is just as moral as the Christian legalist who keeps every one of the commandments with good intentions. Furthermore, if motives (even tender loving care) are the basis for evaluation, then the basic assumption of the new morality is destroyed; namely, that actions should produce results—the greatest good for the greatest number. The best of motives cannot repair damage done by certain acts. Finally, since situationism has no intrinsic values, there would be no way to judge a motive; even hate would be a commendable motive under certain situations.

Once again, the situationist is in a corner from which he would like to escape. Using motives as an arbiter in moral matters is extremely uncomfortable. As noted in chapter 3, the situationist prefers to jump from one epistemological base to another, giving the impression that he can be on several at the same time. Therefore, it is not surprising that Fletcher writes that "no sexual act is ethical if it hurts or exploits others."[4] Now, we are back to the timeworn theory that the basis of sexual conduct rests with the results.

The problems of such an ethic have already been discussed, but consider the following illustration: A man intends to rape a woman but is prevented from doing so because of an unexpected intruder, and the woman escapes unharmed. Another man has a "loving" sexual relationship with a girl whom he does not intend to marry. He has no motive to harm her, and it is agreed that they are not hurting others. Unknown to both of them, the girl contracts venereal disease during the relationship, which in time will cripple her body. Of the two men, which one should be regarded as the more ethical? If Fletcher is right when he says a sexual act is not ethical if it hurts others, then the latter may well be regarded as immoral while the rapist would be moral.

In short, if morality is determined by results, any criminal act would become moral if through some accident or coincidence the consequences turned out for the better, even though the criminal *intended* otherwise. Of course, if pressed, the situationist would like to return to motives once again! But as has already been argued ad nauseam, motives and consequences cancel each other; the situationist is caught by his own trap.

How does situationism work within a social system? If a decision has to be made between legalism and the new morality (that this choice is unnecessary will be shown in chapter 8), legalism would still be preferred. First, situationism does not abolish hypocrisy as it claims. In discussing the Ten Commandments, Fletcher says that it is possible to only *pretend* to have faith in God, if it be for a loving cause. Few legalists have condoned such hypocrisy! In fact, since love can be served through deception, one can never know whether a situationist is telling the truth or not. Perhaps being a hypocrite is necessary to reach a loving goal. This was vividly illustrated in a debate in which Dr. John Warwick Montgomery and Joseph Fletcher participated. Montgomery pointed out that neither he nor the audience could ever know if Fletcher is telling the truth. Montgomery asserted that even if Fletcher swore on his mother's grave *"that very assurance* may well be a situationally justified prevarication for the sake of 'doing us good in love' by convincing us of the merits of situationalism."[5]

There is no reason for a situationist to be honest, since honesty is not intrinsically valuable. As was pointed out, when Fletcher says that honesty should reign, he is falling back into the view that honesty has inherent value. But in situationism, honesty cannot be considered good unless it helps somebody. The new morality by its very nature condones hypocrisy; in fact, it is necessary, especially when love demands it. Admittedly, many legalists are hypocritical and only pretend to observe the rules, but few such systems consider this conduct as the ideal. Situationism, which has no moral absolutes, must of necessity approve of the deceptions that frequently characterize legalism. To assert that the new morality abolishes hypocrisy is in principle fallacious.

There is a second reason why legalism—even the kind Fletcher talks about—is preferable to situationism. A legalistic system can at least produce a stable social structure. Plato recognized this and argued at length in the *Republic* that laws must be enforced if a state is to function. The new morality, if applied universally, would of necessity destroy society. Basil Mitchell comments:

It is hard to see how a society of any complexity could survive or be worth preserving if its members approached their obligations in the spirit of Fletcher's official theory. What would become of the institution of marriage if the marriage vow were taken to mean "I will remain faithful unto you until the situation appears to me to call for adultery"? Or if parental responsibility were interpreted to mean "We will care for you so long as circumstances seem to justify the policy"?[6]

Let us suppose that the official courts of a nation operated on the principle of the new morality. Each law would be subject to change and could be abolished if the purpose of love was being served. Every moral act would be considered neutral; a person would be automatically acquitted if his action (1) brought about greater good for the greater number, and (2) if his motives were loving. (The contradiction between these two methods might be resolved after the fashion of Alice in Wonderland, who could believe as many as six contradictions before breakfast!) The following four illustrations demonstrate how the new morality would operate in actual situations. The first two stories are as yet fictitious (for which all individuals including situationists may well be grateful); but the last two are factual stories, taken from actual "situations."

In Washington a high-ranking government official becomes aware that the political party in power has a foreign policy which is detrimental to the welfare of the country. The President's domestic policy is somewhat more encouraging, but this does not outweigh the harm being done abroad. The official is not partial to either party, since he has been an advisor for a number of different administrations. But having inside information, he is convinced that the President is undermining the prestige of the US, which will eventually lead to the nation's ruin. He cannot convince the President to change, and he believes that the country cannot afford to continue on its present course until the next election. The official is reasonably certain of who would be elected President if both the President and

Vice-President were assassinated; this potential candidate would administer the international affairs in a way that would bring about more good for a greater number.

Making a vast agapeic calculus, he hires a friend to place a bomb under the President's limousine. The plot succeeds; both the President and Vice-President are killed. The country is shocked, and flounders until another administration is elected. Soon after the inauguration, the FBI links the government official with the assassination of the former leaders. The court has adopted the basic tenet of the new morality: every action is morally neutral; only the intention of the agent and the results, that is, the greatest happiness for the greatest number, determine morality. The official is arrested, but after brief deliberation he is set free because (1) the man had good motives, which alone is sufficient to justify an act; (2) the court needed time to determine what foreign policy *is* the best for the nation; and (3) any verdict must be withheld for at least four years to evaluate the performance of the incumbent President. In this way the court could determine whether the new President is bringing about the greatest good for the greatest number.

Several years later, the court still cannot decide whether the government official is guilty of a crime. It was finally agreed that the present President had a more impressive record in handling foreign affairs, and so the court decided to return the verdict of not guilty.

Just then one member of the jury asked, "Is it not true that what is good for America in foreign policy is bad for other countries? Is not the world so constituted that if any nation gets what is good for it, the others do not get what is good for them? If we are really serious about the greatest good for the greatest number, our former President was more ethical. Even if his foreign policy had ruined the nation, it would have increased the happiness of many more millions in foreign countries."

The court adjourned indefinitely. This was indeed a perplexing matter, and it became even more difficult when the chief justice realized that there was no *inherent* reason (despite their formal oaths) why any of the witnesses or jurors should be telling the truth. The case was dropped for lack of information and evidence.

In another part of the nation, a man robbed the home of a wealthy actress. His loot was $600,000 worth of jewelry. Three years later he was caught, and voluntarily confessed that he had taken the merchandise. With the money he had built a new home for his family and sent his children to college. The surplus was invested in a new school being built in the neighborhood. In this instance he was not even brought to trial, because it was not known if his act could be regarded as a crime. Since stealing is neutral, the man was asked about his intentions, and they were found to be loving (of course, the man may have been lying; there is no intrinsic reason why he should be honest just so long as he has the good of others in mind). The only matter still open to question was the results of his act. Obviously, the happiness of this man's family of six was of more value than the prestige of one wealthy individual! The man was honored for doing the right thing.

Encouraged by his success, he later executed a similar loving act, except that this time someone was killed in the robbery. When the assailant was found a few years later, he had used all the stolen money to build a much needed hospital. The court agreed that people should be placed ahead of principles, but this did not settle the matter. Was the life of one individual of more value than the health (and life) of several hundred? The verdict was obvious. The man was again honored for "sinning bravely" as the new moralists encourage people to do. It was evident that more neighbors had been served rather than fewer.

The two following stories are actual situations which demonstrate the perplexity of any moral code based on a contentless love. In Washington, D.C., a young man killed his girl friend.

It wasn't done out of malice; it was a cool, calculated act. Apparently he did this in order to spare her from experiencing something unpleasant. It is difficult to know what Fletcher's opinion of this situation might be. When discussing the value of human life, he writes:

> Death control, like birth control, is a matter of human dignity. Without it persons become puppets. To perceive this is to grasp the error lurking in the notion—widespread in medical circles—that life as such is the highest good. This kind of vitalism seduces its victims into being more loyal to the physical spark of mere biological life than to the personality values of self-possession and human integrity. The beauty and spiritual depths of human stature are what should be preserved and conserved in our value system, with the flesh as the means rather than the end.[7]

Having given such a high priority to human dignity (placing it above human life)—assuming that the boy killed his girl friend to spare her from an ordeal where her "beauty and spiritual depths of human stature" would be destroyed—the court might well decide situationally to let the boy go free. At any rate, it would be impossible to prove that this action was not in keeping with the girl's highest good, unless that good be specifically defined and defended.

Early in 1971 much publicity was given to the Charles Manson trial in California. When asked to testify, Susan Atkins described in detail how she murdered the actress Sharon Tate. Miss Atkins then added,

> I feel no guilt for what I have done. Should I feel remorse or guilt for what I have done? Should I feel remorse or sorry for doing what was right for me? Doing what I know was right for me? What I did was coming from love, to help my brother get out of jail, and anything that comes from love is good. I felt no hatred, no malice. I didn't even know those people. But they were part of the system that jailed my brother for something I did and I was going back on the sys-

tem. It was right then and it's right now. . . . What feels right, feels good.[8]

The following should be noted. If *motives* determine morality, Miss Atkins is surely guiltless; she believed in what she was doing, and it is difficult if not impossible to prove that the murder was not for the greatest good, if Miss Atkins' value system is accepted. The act might lead to the release of her brother from jail, or the publicity of the trial could cause some needed changes in the present court system; and above all, Miss Atkins may believe (could Fletcher disprove it?) that the establishment is so evil that any contribution she can make toward its downfall—including murder—is well worth the price. (Incidentally, in the same speech, she stated that Charles Manson was not connected with the crime. If she was not telling the truth, the situationist would likely approve wholeheartedly, since in that situation it might be the most loving thing to do.) In Miss Atkins' mind, Manson's life, reputation, and teaching may be of incalculable worth. In a relativistic society no one could prove that his philosophy and approach to life are wrong.

At any rate, the trial could not continue on a situational basis until every motive, result, and value system was weighed. The outcome would of necessity be based on personal preference. Perhaps this situation can best be summarized in Fletcherian terminology: "We may or may not agree with Miss Atkins' value system, but no situationist can quarrel with her method of ethical decision."

It is unnecessary to provide other illustrations of what would happen if situation ethics became the accepted standard of morality on a national scale. Every conceivable crime would be committed and would go unpunished, simply because no one could have enough facts to determine what is moral and what is not. (Consider a society in which vote fraud is legitimate, as long as it is done by the party that is best for the people!) It should now be clear that the new morality is not so much wrong as it is completely meaningless. A word like *love* which is compatible with anything and everything is indeed useless as a basis for making moral decisions.

Possibly the clearest statement of the total bankruptcy of any humanistic ethic is that of Ludwig Wittgenstein in his essay in the *Philosophical Review*. Wittgenstein is regarded as one of the leading thinkers in analytical philosophy which concentrates on the problem of meaning and the principle of verification. Wittgenstein believed that all ethical statements were simply statements of fact; there is no judgment that can claim absolute value. This means that a moral system based on the quicksands of relativism can never tell a person what he *ought* to do. Fletcher, who rejects absolutes, would at least agree with Wittgenstein that no *system* of ethics is possible in a humanistic framework; for this reason he prefers to call his ethics a *non*system. He even admits that "we simply cannot climb across the gap from descriptive to prescriptive propositions; from 'is' statements to 'ought' statements. We have to make jumps, faith leaps. They are not steps in logic or even in common sense."[9] The difference between Fletcher and Wittgenstein is that the latter sees the utter meaninglessness of talking about good and evil, since there is no epistemological anchor for such judgments. Wittgenstein realizes that if there are ethical absolutes, they would have to come to man from *outside* of the human situation. Man does not know enough, nor is it possible for him to know enough to build a moral system that will tell him what to do. Thus Wittgenstein writes, "If a man could write a book on Ethics which really was a book on Ethics, this book would, with an explosion destroy all the other books in the world."[10] Wittgenstein saw that ethics cannot be based on the relativistic opinions of man; in order to have an ethical system, man needs help. He adds, "Ethics, if it is anything, is supernatural and our words will express only facts."[11] Wittgenstein did not believe that such a supernatural revelation existed; but he saw clearly that if there was no such help from a supernatural source, all of man's talk about good and evil (we may add, what is loving and what is not) is, in nonphilosophical language, *nonsense*. At best, man can describe facts, but a logical analysis of ethical statements shows that they are all on the same plane. "My conscience tells me to burn a widow with the corpse of her husband," a pagan told a British officer. The officer replied, "My conscience tells me to hang you if you do." Such is the nature of the ethical dilemma. Without an objective standard, morality is simply a matter of personal preference.

But what about Wittgenstein's challenge? Is there a book on ethics that is really a book on ethics? Is there a book with authority that can tell me what I *ought* to do—apart from the consequences? Historic Christianity makes such a claim. The Book upon which it is based answers the questions that situationism cannot answer, and those who live by its precepts need not even be legalistic!

8

A Biblical Alternative

THE AUTHORITY OF CHRIST

CHRISTIANITY ASSERTS that the Bible is the sole authority in matters of religion and ethics. The Old Testament as well as the New is an expression of the will of God for mankind. Jesus Christ is therefore regarded as the final and most complete revelation of God; He claimed that His teaching was from the Father, and His mission was to reveal the Father's will (Jn 7:16, 17:4). It is, of course, possible to reject Christ's authority completely and perhaps even ignore His claims. But it is not possible (unless one can live with intolerable logic) to accept part of His teaching and reject the remainder. Christ cannot be a final authority only in selected subjects. If He was not God as He claimed (Jn 8:58), then indeed He was a liar. And if these statements about Himself are not accurate—if He was mistaken about His own identity—then there is no valid reason to suppose that He was telling the truth in other matters. But if He was who He claimed to be, then every word He spoke becomes significant, and His ethical precepts become *the* basis for moral judgments.

One of the unique features of the new moralists is their anxiousness to have Christ as their supreme example and authority. Bishops Pike and Robinson appeal to Christ as the one who championed the view that love was more important than

75

law, and hence, that love replaces the law in moral issues. Fletcher makes repeated references to Christ as the one who taught that the summary rule of love takes precedence over rules, and people are to be served rather than precepts. In keeping with this, he asserts, "Modern Christians ought not to be naïve enough to accept any other view of Jesus' ethic than the situational one."[1] Even Hugh Hefner cannot resist the lure of being a follower of Christ and occasionally cites Him as *Playboy's* authority. In chapter 4 it was shown that the term *situationism* is so broad that if values are left undefined, even Christ could fit under the label. He did that which He considered the most loving. But the question is Did He have Fletcher's system of values? Did He teach that commandments must sometimes be broken to serve love? Did He adopt a pragmatic and relativistic theory of ethics? In short, was He a situationist in Fletcher's sense of the word?

Spokesmen for the new morality rightly observe that Christ rebelled against the legalism of His day. One incident recorded in the gospels is frequently used to prove Christ's adherence to situation ethics. In Matthew 12:1-8 Christ and His disciples ate corn on the Sabbath. When criticized by the Pharisees, Christ reminded them that David ate showbread unlawfully because he was hungry (1 Sa 21:6). Fletcher uses this incident to show that Jesus was willing to follow the radical decisions of love. He also uses Christ's subsequent words, "The sabbath was made for man, and not man for the sabbath," as evidence of Christ's situationism.[2]

In connection with the entire incident several facts should be noted. First, picking corn on the Sabbath was not forbidden in the Old Testament. The Pharisees had *added* that to the Sabbath law. Carl Henry states, "The elders had added tradition upon tradition to make the sabbath a burdensome religious requirement."[3]

Second, provision was made to work on the Sabbath if it was necessary (Mt 12:11-12; Jn 7:22). Again, Henry writes:

The sabbath did not therefore imply simply an absolute rest. Rather, it implied the cessation of ordinary labor imposed by the demands of man's vocation in order that the higher claims of life might be brought unrestrictedly into view.[4]

Third, Christ's statement regarding the Sabbath (Mk 2:27-28) cannot be regarded as a repudiation of the Sabbath law of the Old Testament. The Sabbath was indeed made for man; he was to worship God and exercise his spiritual life in deeds of love and kindness. *Man* was not made to be a *slave* to Pharisaical requirements; he was to observe the Sabbath so that he would be free from ordinary labor and worship God without restriction.

Fourth, the actual incident in 1 Samuel 21 could be reconstructed as follows: The priest tells David that the bread is holy and therefore illegal for David to eat. David replies that the bread has now become common, for it has been taken from the table and fresh bread has replaced it. Furthermore, David adds that he and the men had not been with women; there is no reason why they should not be permitted to eat the loaves. Then Ahimelech evidently replies that it was the Sabbath, and for this reason David and his men should not eat the bread. David responds by saying that it is not the Sabbath that sanctifies the bread; the bread is sanctified by its being in the dish on the table in the holy place. But since it had been removed, it could be freely eaten. In Matthew 12, Christ referred to this incident because His disciples were accused of breaking the Sabbath; David's actions demonstrated that eating on the Sabbath—even if it is eating bread that had been consecrated —is not wrong. Similarly, picking heads of grain and eating them was not a violation of the Sabbath law. This incident cannot be used to show that Christ approved of breaking Old Testament laws because of expediency.

If Christ's views in matters of morality are regarded as authoritative, it is necessary to examine what His reaction was toward law and love. Without question, Christ repudiated the legalism of the Pharisees, but does this make Him an advocate of a situational ethic? Even though every reader of the New Testament finds love written large on its pages, it is equally obvious that Christ was not expounding an ethic in which every act is neutral and only the results or intention makes it right or wrong. In fact, He did not repudiate the Old Testament law but repeatedly quoted it as authoritative and binding. That Christ was not a Fletcherian situationist can easily be demonstrated.

First, Christ never condemned anyone for adhering to an explicit commandment of the Old Testament. Even in Mark 7:7-15 Christ did not rebuke the Pharisees for fulfilling the Old Testament ceremonial observances. His criticism was directed at those who missed the spiritual message latent in the ceremonial law.

Second, Christ's sharp rebuke against legalism was directed to the Pharisees for adding their *own* regulations to the Old Testament law. He frequently accused them of substituting their own tradition in place of commandments of God (Mk 7:9).

Third, Christ's solution to legalism was a return to obedience to the written record of the Old Testament (Mt 5:19; Jn 5:45-47, 10:35).

Fourth, Christ constantly emphasized that the laws of the Old Testament must be observed with a proper heart attitude (Mk 7:6). Christ's answer to legalism is that *external* obedience to the moral law must be coupled with a corresponding *inner* attitude of love and honesty. Thus Christ's teaching was not intended to abrogate obedience to the moral law, but to add to it its intended spirit. For example, many of the Pharisees legalistically kept the commandment Thou shalt not commit adultery. The solution to this legalism was not to make exceptions to the commandment, but to add to it its inner implications. Jesus said, "Whosoever looketh at a woman to lust after her hath committed adultery with her already in his heart" (Mt 5:28). Fletcher's answer to legalism is to do away with obedience to the letter of the law and merely preserve its "spirit" (if such could be possible!). Christ's solution was to insist on outward obedience to the law *along with* its intended "spirit" or inner implications.

Fifth, even Fletcher must admit that Christ did not follow the utilitarian principle of situationism. When discussing the story of the anointing at Bethany, Fletcher observes that Christ chose the way of uncalculating and unenlightened love. Since Christ did not accept the situationist's decision, Fletcher concludes that "if we take the story as it stands, Jesus was wrong and the disciples were right."[5] This is sufficient evidence that Christ was not a situationist.

Christ's view of love and the law still awaits further explanation. But at this point it is necessary to emphasize that the situationists cannot—and dare not—use Christ as their authority. Such a step involves a theological inconsistency which has devastating results. For example, Christ accepted the Old Testament as authoritative. He vouched for its accuracy and plainly stated, "Whosoever, therefore, shall break one of these least commandments, and shall teach men so, he shall be called the least in the kingdom of heaven; but whosoever shall do and teach them, the same shall be called great in the kingdom of heaven" (Mt 5:19).

Such statements are, of course, anathema to the adherents of the new morality, since a situationist cannot tolerate Christ's acceptance of the absoluteness of the law. Situationists cannot take these verses literally, and hence find alleged contradictions between these statements and others in the gospels and the writings of Paul. The difficulty is that no logical contradictions exist. The Sermon on the Mount is largely an exposition of the Ten Commandments with an emphasis on the intended spirit of the law along with external obedience. Nowhere does

Christ suggest that this teaching is to be situationally applied. Evidence for His acceptance of the totality of the Old Testament as a revelation from God is extensive. Yet in the face of such facts, Bishop Robinson says,

> The moral precepts of Jesus are not intended . . . as prescribing what all Christians must do, whatever the circumstances, and pronouncing certain courses of action universally right and others universally wrong . . . they are illustrations of what love may at any moment require of anyone.[6]

If the words of Christ cannot be taken at face value, and if He did not intend that His moral precepts be universally applied, then it is incumbent upon the new moralists to explain why certain teachings should be taken literally and why others should be rejected. If Christ was ethically mistaken when He condoned the action of Mary when she anointed Him, there is no reason why He was correct about His view of love. To accept a *part* of Christ's teaching as right and other parts as wrong is to reject the basic notion that Christ came to reveal the Father and to give accurate information regarding His will. Essentially, when the situationist evaluates Christ's words—accepting some and discarding others—he is thereby writing his own autobiography. The new moralist's authority rests squarely upon his own shoulders. He decides when Christ was speaking for God and when He was not.

It is, of course, the prerogative of every individual to reject the teachings of Christ. It is possible to take the position that He was self-deceived or a liar. But is it moral to hold either of these two views and still use Christ as a foundation stone in building a moral system (or *non*system)? Possibly, someone may respond by saying that Christ (like an ordinary man) was wrong sometimes and right at others; hence each individual is free to select the part that suits his fancy. But such a conclusion misses the point. If Christ was only a man, there is no reason at all to suggest that His teaching is what we *ought* to fol-

low in any area. There is no reason to recommend Christ over
Aristotle and Plato. Even more serious, if Christ did not speak
the truth in all matters, the claims about Himself vanish like the
idle babbling of a lunatic bent on deceiving the world. Unlike
Plato and Aristotle, He could not afford to be wrong—even
once.

The new morality is an ethical view that wishes to find its
roots in a few selected statements of Christ. These statements
are torn from the context of His total teaching, and whole
chapters are bypassed. It is obvious that such eisegesis results
in what at best can be referred to as a weak and inconsistent
Christology. God is regarded as either dead, gone, or irrelevant. The word *love* is isolated from the remainder of Scripture and permitted to be the mask that justifies any conduct
imaginable. Robinson confidently claims:

> The Sanctions of Sinai have lost their terrors, and people no
> longer accept the authority of Jesus even as a great moral
> teacher. Robbed of its supranatural supports, men find it
> difficult to take seriously a code of living that confessedly
> depended on them . . . Supranaturalistic reasons . . . have
> force and even meaning, for none but a diminishing religious
> remnant.[7]

Where does such a view lead us? It leads us back to a Christ
who is (1) wrong about the existence of a personal God who is
the lawgiver, (2) deceived regarding His own identity, and (3)
mistaken about the Scripture—that is, the Old Testament as an
authoritative revelation. He was correct only on one count:
He summarized the law by saying, "Love your neighbor as
yourself"; and this, His interpreters tell us, means that there are
no inherent moral laws, so do whatever *you* think is most
loving.

Pushed to a logical conclusion, the new moralists would have
to admit that Christ was almost always wrong; only occasionally (perhaps by accident) He spoke the truth. That this is the
necessary conclusion of the teaching of Fletcher became evi-

dent during his debate with John Warwick Montgomery. Fletcher, striving to be consistent, was forced to admit that "Jesus was a simple Jewish peasant. He had no more philosophical sophistication than a guinea pig, and I don't turn to Jesus for philosophical sophistication."[8] Such a remark should not be too surprising despite Fletcher's frequent favorable remarks about Christ. It is the necessary conclusion of anyone who believes that Christ was a crusader for what has become known as the new morality.

It is regrettable that other advocates of the new morality do not make similar statements regarding Christ. This would help to clarify their viewpoint, so that it would in no way become confused with biblical ethics. While consistency would demand such confessions of faith (or *non*faith), the new moralists have frequently been reluctant to make such clear statements regarding the person of Christ. The only possible reason why such frank confessions are not forthcoming must lie within the framework of the new morality itself. Situationally it is moral to give people the *impression* that the new morality is the teaching of Christ, if greater good is accomplished (i.e., that more people become situationists). Such deception must be thought necessary to give the new morality needed support. Only when pressed for consistency does the veneer of "we follow Christ" fade and vanish. When honesty reigns, Jesus Christ turns out to be as ignorant as "a guinea pig." Until such a dramatic moment of truth, He is misinterpreted, used, and mutilated. A guinea pig indeed!

A man was driving past a farmyard when he noticed a sight that drew his immediate attention. On one side of the farmer's barn were numerous targets, and in the center of each one—right in the bull's-eye—there was an arrow. He was astonished to think that anyone could be such an expert marksman. He decided to stop his car and congratulate the farmer for his precision in using a bow and arrow. The farmer was unimpressed. "That was not done by me," he explained. "That was done by the village idiot. He comes out here, takes his bow, and shoots arrows into the side of the barn; and then he paints the targets around them!"

The new moralists have their bow and arrow too. No attempt is made to aim for (much less hit) God's target. Everyone is permitted to shoot his arrow wherever he wishes. "God" (i.e., love), then comes along and paints the targets around the arrow. There is one advantage to this method: Each one may do whatever he wishes, and at the same time piously insist that he is doing the will of God.

THE BIBLICAL CONTENT OF LOVE

Written large on the pages of both the Old and the New Testament is the word *love*. There can be no quarrel with the new moralists that God intends that a man love his neighbor and seek the good of others. However, the new morality and biblical morality part when the problem is raised regarding the *content* of love. Whereas the new moralists think that love must be defined by human beings and tailored to meet each situation, biblical writers hold that love is served by keeping the commandments of God. The world has no resources for the construction of normative judgments. God alone can determine morality, and as the divine Legislator, He expects man to obey His laws. Love is not left undefined.

Even before the fall of man in Eden, man did not possess an intuitive knowledge of the divine will of God. Undoubtedly, Adam and Eve had a moral sense and knew that they were to respond to God. But even though the law was engraved on their hearts, this was insufficient in determining all of God's precepts. Ironically, contemporary situationists believe that fallen man has the ability to know what God's will is quite apart from any laws. Yet, in the Scriptures, Adam and Eve were given specific instruction before sin had marred their moral consciousness. If there was any place where love alone should have been able to instinctively tell man what to do, it would have been in the Garden of Eden. Selfishness had not yet entered the heart of man; and presumably with a limited number of people, the consequences could have been easily calculated. Yet God did not allow Adam to decide what was moral; such decisions can only come from the Almighty.

For this reason God gave man specific commands. He was to (1) replenish the earth, (2) subdue the earth, (3) take care of the garden, and (4) be careful not to eat of the tree of the knowledge of good and evil (Gen 1:28, 2:15-17). Admittedly, a number of the commands had a social emphasis, and many details of conduct were omitted. However, the point is that even Adam could not discern God's will without rules. If the *imago Dei* was not sufficient to give unfallen man clear guidance, it assuredly is not sufficient to serve as a moral guide for fallen, sinful man. In Romans, Paul speaks of man as not only alienated from God but also in rebellion against His authority. There is none that seeks after God, there is none that does good (Ro 3:11-12). If there is one dominant characteristic of fallen man, it is rebellion against God. As a result, he does not have the ability nor desire to love his neighbor as himself. This does not mean that unregenerate man can have no capacity whatever for human love. Jesus implied that an evil man can show a measure of love. "If ye then, being evil, know how to give good gifts unto your children, how much more shall your heavenly Father give the Holy Spirit to them that ask him" (Lk 11:13). However, such love is unacceptable before God, and it is not a complete guide for fulfilling moral obligations.

At Sinai, God spelled out the moral law in greater detail than in previous revelations. In the Ten Commandments and numerous other commands, the Israelites had little doubt as to what God demanded. Subsequently, the nation was judged repeatedly for its failure to keep the law which God had given. The scathing denunciation of the prophets was directed to people who had begun to do what was right in their own eyes. But even at this time neighbor-love was emphasized (Lev 19:18).

Christ's moral teaching was based on the Old Testament. As already indicated, He rejected the legalism of the Pharisees but at the same time did not relax one moral precept of the Old Testament. His summary statement of the law does not mean that all commandments are now passé. He said, "Thou shalt love the Lord, thy God, with all thy heart, and with all thy soul, and with all thy mind. This is the first and great commandment. And the second is like it, Thou shalt love thy neighbor as thyself" (Mt 22:37-39).

Several observations should be noted. First, these words are quoted directly from the Old Testament (Deu 6:5; Lev 19:18). This reminds us that Christ did not reject the authority of the Old Testament in matters of morality. He was not suggesting that a new commandment of love was to replace the former precepts which God had given. Second, the commandment is best understood if the imperative force is applied to both neighbor-love and self-love. Then the idea is that one should love his neighbor as he *ought* to love himself. This would emphasize that man is incapable even of proper self-love, much less neighbor-love. There is no contradiction within the teaching of Scripture, when on the one hand men are commanded to love themselves, and on the other hand God regards natural self-love as unacceptable (2 Ti 3:1-2). As a creature created in God's image, man should see himself as valuable and have a proper respect for himself. But because of sin, man's self-love has become distorted and selfish; this is what God condemns. It is only when he is regenerated that man's self-love acquires its proper perspective.

Third, there is a relationship between love for God and love for one's neighbor. But the relationship is not the one suggested by Fletcher, namely, that one loves God by loving his neighbor. The reverse is true. One cannot love his neighbor unless he loves God. Godet points out that the last part of the summary is directly dependent upon the first. He writes,

"Nothing but the reigning love of God can so divest the individual of devotion to his own person, that the ego of his neighbor shall rank in his own eyes exactly on the same level as his own."[9] God changes sinful self-love into regenerated self-love; then with additional supernatural help, one is able to love his neighbor as himself. Fourth, the content of neighbor-love is given specifically in the Scriptures. Possibly the clearest statement occurs in Romans 13:8-10. Verse eight reads, "Owe no man any thing, but to love one another; for he that loveth another hath fulfilled the law." This verse is frequently quoted by Fletcher to demonstrate that Paul was also a situationist, since love is the only imperative mentioned here. Conveniently, Fletcher does not quote the succeeding verses: "For this, Thou shalt not commit adultery, Thou shalt not kill, Thou shalt not steal, Thou shalt not bear false witness, Thou shalt not covet; and if there be any other commandment, it is briefly comprehended in this saying, namely, Thou shalt love thy neighbor as thyself. Love worketh no ill to its neighbor; therefore, love is the fulfilling of the law" (Ro 13:9-10).

Here, as in countless other instances, love is commanded along with the injunctions of the law. More simply, love is *defined* as obedience to law. Note specifically that Paul and Christ teach that love *fulfills* the law rather than *replaces* it. The Scriptures also teach that Christ came to redeem us from the curse of the law (Gal 3:13). But this is not intended to imply that the law no longer represents God's standard of morality. It simply means that the law should not be considered as a means of acquiring righteousness before God. The law is a schoolmaster to bring us to Christ (Gal 3:24); and since no man has kept it perfectly, each one is driven to the cross for forgiveness. Having been forgiven, those who yield to the Spirit will discover that the righteousness of the law is fulfilled in them (Ro 8:4). God therefore has given man a standard which is beyond human ability, but Christ fulfilled

God's requirements so that man can be pronounced righteous (Ro 3:21-31). We are made the righteousness of God *in Him.* But God's moral standard has not changed. The commandments in Scripture are clear enough for guidance in the everyday decisions of life.

If, therefore, the content of love is spelled out in Scripture, the question that arises is Why did God choose *these* particular commandments? Was His choice arbitrary? To begin with, it should be noted that there is no moral rule outside of God to which He must be subject. God can, if He wishes, legislate moral laws and at times abrogate them if He so wishes (this may partly explain Kierkegaard's paradox regarding Abraham who was asked to slay his son). But it is incorrect to think of the commandments as arbitrary, that is, as though the precepts God chose were simply selected at random and therefore, one could have been chosen just as easily as another. The moral laws of God are basically a *reflection* of His own character; hence, "Be ye holy; for I am holy" (1 Pe 1:16).

Such a view rids us of the notion that God gave the laws without any specific reason. Young people particularly have suspected that God revealed certain laws merely because He wanted to take the fun out of life. God is pictured as one who cannot tolerate people on earth who have a good time. Such an opinion is wide of the mark. Since God is an omniscient Creator, He knows which rules are best for mankind; and these moral laws are a reflection of His nature, imposed on a universe which He created—a universe which functions best when His laws are obeyed.

An illustration might help. If one were to make a machine (better yet, think of man as creating it), he would know how the machine could reach its highest state of performance and hence he would give instructions that would implement that end. Such rules would be directed toward a predetermined goal. Also, the rules would reflect the nature of the machine's creator. His goals, designs, and values would be in view. Similarly, God has a certain purpose He wishes to achieve, and part of His plans include instructions for mankind.

At this point the discussion returns to the question of whether an ethic should be based on consequences. This book was written to expose the fallacies of any ethic which judges morality by human calculation. If man cannot build an ethic which is calculating and designed to achieve certain consequences, can God? The answer is yes.

There is one remark in Fletcher's book that agrees in toto with biblical teaching. In defending the view that the end justifies the means, Fletcher reminds his readers that the problem of evil has often been resolved by the theory that God uses evil to bring about some greater purpose. He concludes, "Here is a theodicy based squarely on the view that the end justifies the means."[10] Christian theologians have maintained for centuries that as a sovereign ruler, God has the right to do as He wishes to bring about desired results. Possibly the strongest assertion of such a doctrine is Proverbs 16:4, "The LORD hath made all things for himself; yea, even the wicked, for the day of evil." Can one conceive of God creating the world for no purpose whatever? Did He create man without any predetermined end in view? Is evil simply an intruder over which He had no control, or is there a purpose in it too?

The consistent teaching of Scripture is that God is the sovereign ruler who can do what He wishes in the army of men and among the inhabitants of the earth. He can use any means available to achieve a desired end. Suppose He has one goal in mind—His own glory, for instance. Such an end would not be immoral. God has no one to whom He is subject. There is no law outside of Himself to which He must bow. For Him, the end does justify the means. And, of course, one of the means He may use to accomplish His purpose is to give man specific instructions regarding moral conduct. These universal absolute moral laws are to be kept at all times, regardless of the circumstances. Thus it is man's responsibility to obey, and when he does, God controls the consequences. Since He is sovereign, He can turn even the most undesirable results into a greater good. This is done so deftly that even the wrath of man ends up praising Him.

As has already been argued, man cannot play the part of God. Since for the situationists, the transcendent God is dead or irrelevant, it is believed that man must replace Him. The results are disastrous. God alone knows all the facts, sets all the goals, and determines morality. Nowhere in Scripture are His principles to be replaced in favor of *human* calculation. He allows us to play the game; He does not allow us to make the rules.

Perhaps it is significant that the first sin committed was the result of situation ethics. When Adam and Eve saw the fruit, it looked good for food; it was pleasant to the eyes and a fruit to be desired to make one wise. Ignoring God's direct prohibition, they thought there was nothing inherently right in commandments themselves. Maybe they thought it naïve to obey a law simply because God said so. So, thinking that they had adequately evaluated the consequences—having reasoned that there could be nothing wrong with food (fruit)—they made an agapeic calculus and ate the fruit. But the results were far more disastrous than they had imagined. Sin entered the human race. The man, woman, and serpent were cursed. Later their son Cain killed their firstborn son Abel and thereby provided the pattern the human race has followed ever since. Why? Because a man and a woman thought morality could be judged by the consequences, and thought *they* had the ability to calculate and predict them.

Note carefully that in this instance, the goals Adam and Eve had in mind were not corrupt. They wanted to be like God (that should qualify as a good intention), and they wanted food. But because they were limited by time and knowledge, they could not predict the catastrophe which awaited them.

Likewise, modern man loosed from restrictions, wishes to be like the Almighty. He will determine what is valuable and what is not; he will snatch from God the throne and scepter, he will be like the Most High. But can he be confident that in the sleep of death no unpleasant dreams may come? Can he calculate the *eternal* results?

Again we return to Wittgenstein's remark that a book on ethics will indeed have to come from outside of the universe. Man cannot predict the next five minutes, much less can he look into eternity; therefore, a book on ethics must of necessity be supernatural.

THE EXAMPLE OF CHRIST

For the Christian, Christ is the supreme example of how the moral life is to be lived. His life represents an ideal which all men should emulate as far as possible. Christ is the only one who claimed to be sinless and no one refuted His charge (Jn 8:46). He was neither a legalist nor a situationist in the sense that new moralists use these terms. Since He does not fit into any of the three ethical categories described by Fletcher, it might be helpful to determine more about His ethical conduct. His life and teaching point to a fourth category, that is, a distinct harmony between love and law.

Christ claimed that He was under the authority of His Father's commandments. He urged the disciples to keep His commandments as He kept the commandments of the Father. "If ye keep my commandments, ye shall abide in my love, even as I have kept my Father's commandments, and abide in his love" (Jn 15:10).

Christ stands as a paramount example of one who was loving, yet exercised His love within the framework of absolute law. When Fletcher makes a Christian choose between legalism and situationism, the choice is unjustified. Not all those who obey the biblical commandments can be classified as "legalistic" and hence have "lost touch with the headaches and heartbreaks of life."[11] Even John Macquarrie who is generally sympathetic with the new morality acknowledges that "the legalism attacked by advocates of the new morality seems to me to have been often a straw man."[12]

It should be evident that law is not wrong in itself. The purpose of the law is to define right and wrong. Legalism is an abuse of the law. It results when law is used to minimize obligation by those who do not go beyond its external requirements, and when it is used as a means of self-righteousness by those who think they can obtain salvation by it. Those who keep the law only outwardly are legalists; those who keep the same law outwardly with a correct heart attitude are not legalists. Legalists keep the law for self-glory, or to merit some reward; they do not keep it because it expresses the desire of their heart. In short, legalism consists in assigning a *wrong function* to law. To solve the problem of legalism by doing away with the law has disastrous results. From a Christian perspective there is no conflict between law and love, because love is defined as obedience to law. As the apostle John wrote, "And this is love, that we walk after his commandments" (2 Jn 6). Elsewhere in the Scriptures, Christians are commanded to love others as Christ loved them (Jn 13:34). This presupposes a knowledge of *how* He loved the world. He did so by obeying the blueprint given by the Father; this is the same way Christians are to love the world. Such obedience is not legalism. It is the Christian's way to love God first and then love his neighbor as himself.

As previously indicated, Christ's solution to legalism was to insist that external obedience to the moral law must be united with the proper inner attitude. The commandment Thou shalt not kill still retains its full force; but along with it, Christ says that the one who hates his brother is a murderer in his heart. The same is true of adultery. To interpret Christ's remarks as meaning that murder and adultery are only sinful in certain situations is clearly false.

Christ's emphasis on intentions reminds us that God demands more than mere external obedience to His precepts. Man looks on the outward appearance, but God looks on the heart. Peter Abelard was correct when he insisted that a deed should be judged by a person's intentions. He erred however in failing to define what constitutes a "good" intention. As a result, murder, adultery, and disobedience to God had to be judged as morally appropriate, simply because the content of a good intention was unspecified. He could have avoided the error of condoning those who crucified Christ, if he would have clarified what counts for a good intention and what does not.

Briefly, a good intention justifies a moral act if the intention is in harmony with biblical commands. For example, if you should be invited to the home of friends for dinner and unintentionally be served poisonous soup, your hostess would not be guilty of murder. Since biblical morality is not determined by consequences, the disastrous results would not make the unintentional mistake immoral. In this instance, the hostess had intentions which are in harmony with biblical commands— kindness to friends, and so on. Because of these intentions, she would be guiltless. However, if it was her intention to poison you, in God's eyes she would be guilty of murder even if you happened to survive the ordeal.

Note carefully that an intention can only make an act righteous if the intention is consistent with biblical morality. Since those who crucified Christ had intentions which were unscriptural (murdering a man without a fair trial, bringing false witness, rejecting the evidence for Christ's deity, etc.), they were guilty even if they *thought* that they were doing right. Contrary to both Abelard and Fletcher, those who crucified Christ committed sin despite their "good" intentions. For this reason Christ prayed, "Father, forgive them for they know not what they do." Likewise those who kill Christians and *think* they are doing the will of God will not be guiltless.

Christian morality solves the problem which situationism

faces unsuccessfully. Situationism must make the impossible choice of finding the criterion for morality either in the intention or the results. If it chooses results, it is plagued by such criticisms as found in earlier chapters of this book. If it chooses intention it must face the problem of which intentions are acceptable and which ones are not; otherwise all types of conduct must be condoned. If the phrase "good intentions" is not given specific content, even Hitler could not be judged immoral. Biblical morality specifies the content of acceptable motivation. What the Almighty sees in the heart must be in harmony with His revealed precepts.

External obedience alone cannot make an act acceptable to God. The young ruler who came to Christ was immoral, even though he tried to keep the law outwardly. Inwardly he was covetous, and this violates a clear command. It was right that he keep the commandments, but only when his motives also were right would his action be acceptable to God. However, because man is a sinner and since God's standards are perfection, man needs divine help. Therefore, Christ promised the power to live righteously to those who depended upon Him. Furthermore, since Christ met God's standards of perfection, each individual must receive Him in order to obtain a right standing before God.

Fletcher holds that a codeless love is the only alternative to a loveless code, but this is not the teaching of Christ, who told His disciples that their love for Him must be proved by their obedience to His will. "If ye love me, keep my commandments" (Jn 14:15). Those who live according to this rule are not legalistic.

THE ABILITY TO ACT LOVINGLY

Apart from philosophical considerations, a further weakness of situationism is the problem of the human dilemma; namely, man by himself does not have the power to act for the good of his neighbor. Fletcher entertains the naïve assumption that if men are told to live selflessly, they will. Motives weigh heavily in situationism, and it is generally assumed that an individual's motives are of the highest order. Thus Fletcher can praise the Rainmaker who makes love to a lonely girl in the barn at midnight. His intention is to restore her sense of womanliness and her hopes for marriage. Fletcher names the Rainmaker as the cohero of his book (a St. Louis cabdriver is the hero). The prostitute in the movie *Never on Sunday* is also to be complimented, according to Fletcher. She finds a young sailor who is afraid he cannot function sexually, and hence suffers from doubt and lack of identity. The woman "manages things deliberately (i.e., responsibly) so that he succeeds with her and gains his self-respect and psychic freedom from a potential fixation on sex itself."[13]

It has already been stressed that Fletcher makes no effort to calculate all the results of sexual experiences. But since both of these events took place in movies, the consequences need not be pressed. The point is that Fletcher regards these episodes as examples of loving behavior. Whether the Rainmaker and the prostitute *used* their victims for self-gratification is not considered as part of the agapeic calculation.

Recently in a book review, a writer evaluated a book on sexual etiquette for women, which gives detailed instructions on how to have illicit love affairs. At one point it discusses the type of partner that should be sought for this extramarital adventure. After listing several potential prospects, it concludes by admonishing women to choose "someone with *more* to lose from exposure than you." *That* is human love at work. It tells a partner, "I love you," but it means, "I love myself—I want you." It wants a relationship where the other partner has more to lose. It is this disregard for the selfish, egoistic motives of the human race that makes situationism a naïve and unworkable theory. Fletcher's view of loving actions can be used to justify any selfish desire. Richard Wurmbrand is right when he says,

The language of love and the language of seduction are the same. The one who wishes a girl for a wife and the one who wishes her for the night in order to throw her away afterwards, both say, "I love you." Jesus told us to distinguish the language of seduction from the language of love, and to tell the wolves clad in sheepskin from the real sheep.[14]

The biblical view of man is that he is depraved and sinful. He has of himself no capacity to act lovingly in the sight of his Creator. He not only has to be told what love is, but he needs the power to act in harmony with love, as it is defined for him. Jesus said, "For out of the heart proceed evil thoughts, murders, adulteries, fornications, thefts, false witness, blasphemies" (Mt 15:19). Situationism begins with man and ends with him. It assumes that he is able to pull himself up without supernatural help. Jesus taught that the first commandment was to love God. Only then can neighbor-love be realized. The Bible spells out the content of love and also provides the dynamic to meet its requirements (Ro 5:5). Man needs a new heart. He must be changed from the inside out. When he becomes a new creation, his capacity for loving obedience is enlarged, and only then can he love God and his neighbor as himself. "Wherefore if any man is in Christ, he is a new creature: the old things are passed away; behold, they are become new" (2 Co 5:17, ASV).

9

Moral Conflicts

IN ANY DISCUSSION of biblical ethics, the question arises as to what type of conduct is pleasing to God when the demands of love and law *seem* to be acutely at variance. The lie of the harlot Rahab is usually given as an example of a sin which was appropriate under the circumstances. Fletcher's ethics is for the most part built on such unusual cases. John Macquarrie notes the fallacy of using the unusual cases as a basis for an ethical theory; he says, "An ethic cannot be built on exceptions. Indeed, hard cases can be recognized only because there is already a tacit assumption of norms."[1] J. P. Mackey fittingly writes, "We all know that there are 'hard cases,' but we must also be aware of the legal adage: Hard cases make bad law."[2]

What applies to law applies to ethics. An ethical philosophy must be able to deal first with the usual, common, ethical decisions. Fletcher errs in assuming that if there is one case where an exception might be made, this permits a general rule. For example, the case of Mrs. Bergmeier is a situation in which adultery may be regarded by some as an appropriate moral choice (that this is not the biblical position will yet be shown). However, even if it was appropriate in *that* situation, it would be wrong to make a general rule from the case. Yet, Fletcher does not just approve of adultery when a mother's relationship with her family is at stake. He says, "Whether any form of sex (hetero, homo or auto) is good or evil depends on whether love is fully served."[3] He also approves of wife-swapping and prostitution. Fletcher assumes that if there can be one exception to a moral rule, then that exception proves that the rule should no longer be used as a standard for ethical conduct.

The mere fact that there are moral conflicts does not prove that situationism is the correct ethical philosophy. As Macquarrie observed, the conflicts remind us that there *are* ethical norms. To assume, as Fletcher does, that situationism solves the problem of conflicts because it is not bound by rules is fallacious.

There are, of course, many illustrations in Fletcher's writings where no genuine moral conflicts exist. For example, he observed that if you could rescue only Da Vinci's Mona Lisa or a baby from a burning building, the personalist would take the baby.[4] Certainly this would be the Christian thing to do. However in this case there would be emotional conflict (no one would want to see the Mona Lisa destroyed), but there would be no genuine moral conflict. No one would be held guilty for not recovering the picture.

Similarly, when a doctor discovers there is only enough plasma for one patient, and therefore he must choose (with deep anguish and regret) between a mother of three and a skid-row drunk, he would probably choose the mother. But in making such a decision, he has not done evil.[5] He did not cause the death of the drunk; given the situation, he could not have prevented it. In such a case, the doctor did not do the lesser of two evils; he did not do evil at all. He is not accountable for a tragedy beyond his control.

There are many other moral conflicts which are not so easily resolved. If one holds that there are universals, what happens when they appear to conflict? Broadly, there are two positions (both of which accept moral absolutes) which attempt a solution to these dilemmas. The first of these holds that absolutes can sometimes be intentionally broken without sin; the second holds that absolutes can never be intentionally broken without committing a sin.

The term *hierarchicalism* refers to a moral theory which holds that ethical norms exist in such an arrangement that each norm is in itself binding; but when a conflict arises, we are exempt from a lower norm in order that we might fulfill a higher obligation. Thus while hierarchicalism accepts the existence of universal norms, it recognizes that some are more important than others. And since an individual is exempt from the lower norm in favor of the higher, each norm must be weighed according to some scale of values.

Norman L. Geisler, in his book *Ethics: Alternatives and Issues*, argues for this position and asserts that it is able to cope with the exceptional cases where ethical principles conflict. Using the illustration of Comdr. Lloyd Bucher who signed false confessions in order to save his crew, Geisler writes:

> According to ethical hierarchicalism, it was right for him to lie (i.e. to intentionally falsify) in order to perform the greater good of saving these many lives. The norm against lying was not destroyed but it was dethroned by a higher obligation. Truth-telling was temporarily suspended but not revoked.[6]

Hierarchicalism does not accept the view that we must sometimes choose the lesser of two evils. When one is faced with a decision where ethical norms conflict, obedience to the higher principle takes precedence over the lower, and therefore no guilt results. As Geisler asks, "Why should a man who chooses the *best* of his available alternatives be held guilty for performing an *evil*, even if it is considered a lesser and forgivable evil?"[7]

Such a solution seems attractive, but it is fraught with numerous difficulties. Geisler is aware of the objections which could be raised and attempts to answer them. First, how can one determine the hierarchy of values? We have already argued that people make ethical decisions on the basis of their value systems; and since little agreement exists as to what is valuable and what is not, there is no consensus in moral matters. Geisler disagrees. He thinks that intuition itself is sufficient to show that the only consistent, ethical positions are variations of a love ethic built upon the intrinsic value of persons. He affirms, "Rather than being vastly or totally different, most ethical creeds are quite similar. And at the core of their similarity is some kind of love norm."[8] Such a statement is defensible only if the content of love is undefined. But if the word is given specific content, radical differences between ethical theories become evident.

Apparently Geisler himself is aware that he is being too generous in evaluating other ethical theories. He therefore adds, "Even *if* some men or some creeds would not recognize some form of the love principle, nevertheless they *ought* to do so. That is to say, they are morally inconsistent for not believing that they ought to love others."[9] Even if this statement be granted, it would be difficult if not impossible to demonstrate that such an appeal to intuition would be sufficient to build a Christian hierarchical value system. Specifically: Would it be possible to show that adultery is evil, on the basis of intuition? Or even on the basis of what Geisler calls the "value of personhood?" Humanists regard sex as an essentially harmless pleasure which should be regulated only by personal taste and preference. Given a humanistic system of values, there would be no rationale whatever for sexual purity. One could commit adultery and wish that others would too. There would be no contradiction in such a conclusion.

Geisler further maintains that all men know intuitively that it is better to love God than man; and even if they don't believe in God, they still have ultimate values and, "Whenever men have ultimate values in view, then they see (or *ought* to that the ultimately valuable is more valuable than what is ‚ ᵴ than ultimately valuable."¹⁰ Such a remark is, of course, true but trivial. Admittedly, Marx, Nietzsche, Hefner, Mohammed, and Christ ordered their lives according to what they believed to be the ultimately valuable. They also agreed that that which was ultimately valuable was of more value than the less valuable. But this did not mean that they agreed on what is in fact valuable and what is not.

The point is, is man capable of determining what is ultimately valuable on his own? The conflicts between proposed ethical theories—both past and present—suggest that the answer is no. If Christ is right, countless others have been wrong. Those who reject revelation may on occasion adopt some values which are identical to Christian values, but when this occurs it is because the law of God is written on their heart; it is not, as Geisler suggests, because some have worked out a rational system that is more consistent. Since the difficulties of working out such a system have already been discussed in earlier chapters of this book, the matter needs no further discussion here.

Geisler, however, accepts the Scriptures as an authoritative revelation from God and claims that the Scriptures themselves support the hierarchical theory. Christ taught that there were some sins which were greater than others. Standing before Pilate He said, "Therefore, he that delivered me unto thee has the greater sin" (Jn 19:11); He also spoke of the weightier matters of the law. Paul speaks of love as being the *greatest* virtue. There is no doubt that the Scriptures teach that all sins are not equal. Some are more serious than others. But does this support hierarchicalism?

If the term be simply taken to mean that some sins are smaller (or greater) than others, the answer is yes. However, this is not what Geisler means by hierarchicalism; he means that when one is confronted by a choice of evils, and he chooses the lesser evil, he has not done evil at all. He writes that "in hierarchicalism, one is not guilty for breaking a lower norm but has an *exemption* from it in view of the overriding duty to the higher norm."[11] But while the New Testament does teach that some sins are smaller than others, even the small ones are *still sins*. Nowhere is there any indication in the Scriptures that sin has not been committed when a moral law was violated because someone was acting with a higher norm in view.*

There are, however, a few illustrations in Scripture which might lend themselves to the view that moral laws are suspended in special circumstances. Geisler cites the story of Abraham and Isaac as a classic example of a conflict of moral principles. Contrary to Kierkegaard, hierarchicalism holds that the moral law forbidding murder was suspended for a higher moral law.[12] But the story of Abraham does not prove the hierarchical position. Admittedly, he did not do the lesser of two evils in his willingness to slay his son, but we must note that God explicitly commanded Abraham to sacrifice his son. Christian theology has always held that God has the prerogative to suspend or even revoke a previous law which He has given. If in exceptional cases He wishes to interfere directly, He has that right. Hierarchicalism would hold that *man* has the right to choose which law should be suspended and when. Also, the story itself is not an explicit account of the universal Thou shalt not kill being transcended. Admittedly, Abraham intended to kill Isaac, but God intervened so that the *act* was not carried out. At any rate, the story of Abraham is a special case and can hardly be used as evidence that in present-day experiences moral laws are temporarily suspended because a higher law supersedes them.

*It has been suggested that Mt 12:5 supports hierarchicalism: "Or have ye not read in the law, how that on the sabbath days the priests in the temple profane the sabbath, and are blameless?" But the point of the passage is simply that God, in the Old Testament, commanded priests to kill animals on the Sabbath (Num 28:8-9). Christ is not suggesting that the priests break one commandment because of another; He is simply asking His critics if they had read what was explicitly commanded in the law. Priests who profaned the Sabbath by killing animals were blameless, because they were doing what God had prescribed.

Other passages are sometimes given to show that lying is right under certain circumstances. God blessed the Hebrew midwives who evidently lied to the king of Egypt (Ex 1:18-20). But the king apparently accepted their explanation as to why they did not kill the male Hebrew babies. It is probable that the Hebrew women bore children without the aid of midwives; the midwives were telling part of the truth. But even if their reply was totally false, there is no evidence that the lie was approved by God. God blessed the midwives because they feared Him, and not because of their falsification of truth. A similar situation is that of Rahab the harlot who told a lie when she hid the spies. Subsequently, in Scripture she is praised for het *faith* and not the lie which she told (Heb 11:31; Ja 2:25). A study of such passages nowhere indicates that those who lie are not guilty because of some higher law.†

Hierarchicalism cannot answer the question of how the hierarchy of values is to be determined. To appeal to intuition is inadequate; an appeal to the Scriptures may aid in establishing some sort of hierarchy among sins and virtues, but the sins remain sins and the virtues remain virtues. There is no evidence that a higher norm makes one exempt from a lower one.

A second problem with hierarchicalism is the question of how a norm can be transcended and still be a universal. Geisler correctly notes that his view will be criticized for wanting to have its cake (of ethical absolutes) and eat it too (i.e., be able to break them for higher norms).[13] His answer in brief is, "When one obeys a higher norm in favor of a lower and opposing one, he is not really breaking the lower one but transcending it. He is not making an exception to the lower norm but getting an exemption from it in view of a superior obliga-

---

†The fact that God frequently uses an immoral event for His own purposes, does not in any way indicate His approval of that act. God is sovereign, so He can take all acts and use them for good. This is most clearly demonstrated at the cross: those who crucified Christ were guilty of malicious murder; yet that event is the basis for God's grace extended to mankind. It could hardly be argued that those who crucified Christ did not sin because God used the crucifixion to save mankind.

tion."[14] The contradiction, then, is presumably solved by substituting the word *transcending* for *breaking* and *exemption* for *exception*. If a person violates a universal law in favor of a higher law, he is not guilty of a transgression. He has not *broken* a law but *transcended* it; he has not made an *exception*, but rather he has been *exempted* from the universal. But does the substitution of these words solve the dilemma?

Geisler continues his explanation by stating that hierarchicalism holds that the absolutes from God are only absolute in a given context, and therefore the theory is a form of contextual absolutism.[15] But if absolutes are only absolutes in certain situations, then of course they are not absolutes. If one can lie or commit adultery without sinning because of an obligation to a higher norm, then clearly these two commandments do not have universal application. To strengthen his arguments, Geisler states that the validity and strength of the moral law is there even when it is being broken, that is, transcended. Yet, if it is there all the time, in what sense is the law not broken if it is not obeyed? And if one can be exempt from one universal in favor of another, how does such an exemption differ from an exception? To substitute one set of terms for another hardly solves the problem. Despite the initial plausibility of Geisler's explanation, the charge that hierarchicalism wants to have its cake and eat it too still stands. If one is guilty of violating a universal norm, we must conclude that he has *broken* the universal and has not merely been *exempted* from it.

If we are free to break universal commands because of the demands of higher ones, the responsibility of determining what is moral and what is not rests with man. In this regard there is some similarity between hierarchicalism and situationism. It would be unfair, however, to suggest that the two views are essentially the same. At least on paper the differences are considerable. Situationism has only one ethical norm—love. Hierarchicalism is not based on relativism but has many ethical norms which have *intrinsic* validity. Furthermore, it does not accept what is commonly meant by The end justifies the means, and it is not utilitarian.‡ Geisler writes, "It is not utilitarian *ends* which can justify lying, but hierarchical *norms* can justify it."[16]

But given these differences, if lower principles are to be broken (or transcended) in favor of higher ones, there would be a great similarity between situationism and hierarchicalism in practice. The reasons for certain actions might be different, but in many instances the results would be the same. Mrs. Bergmeier might well be exempt from the seventh commandment, Thou shalt not commit adultery, because of a higher one, namely, the responsibility a mother has to take care of her family. The hierarchicalist would have to agree with Fletcher that even prostitutes *could* be doing a good thing if the survival of their family depended on it. The seventh commandment would be broken (transcended), and they would have an exemption from it because of a higher norm. Consistent with hierarchicalism, Geisler states: "One may be obliged to engage in sexual intercourse outside of his own marriage in order to save a life. Such would be the greatest good in that situation. Surely the refusal to save a life (or lives) by way of sex would not be right."[17]

Every imaginable form of cheating would be good and right, as long as it was done with deference to a higher principle. Students would have a habit of finding such principles rapidly! Since Geisler suggests that "one should always yield to those courses of action which make for better personal relationships,"[18] the possibility of a greatly disrupted personal relationship would justify a student's moral actions. If a better (higher) norm were needed, he could appeal to the need for a

‡In divorcing hierarchicalism from utilitarianism, Geisler escapes the difficulty of using consequences to determine morality. However, a hierarchicalist must of necessity calculate results before acting. One would never break a lower norm in favor of a higher unless there was some reason to believe that certain desirable results would follow. Even if norms are broken because of principles rather than consequences, the motive for breaking a commandment is utilitarian, i.e., to achieve greater good. In this sense hierarchicalism and utilitarianism cannot be separated.

job in order to live. Surely laws against cheating must be "transcended" for the higher principle of survival. Politicians would be "exempt" from principles of honesty, as long as their party followed the highest principles of the hierarchical arrangement. If they were convinced that their party alone could save the country from certain fate, vote fraud would be legitimate—and moral. All such decisions would not be based on utilitarian ends, but the higher principles of the value of personhood would be the cause for being exempt from the lower norms.

Hierarchicalism attempts to solve the problem of moral conflicts by suggesting that one higher ethical absolute makes an individual exempt from a lower absolute. Its difficulty is that it cannot base its hierarchical arrangement on intuition; nor does such a view find sanction in the Scriptures. It accepts the existence of universals as being only contextually universal and assumes that the responsibility of deciding when and how the commands should be broken (transcended) rests with man. While such a view can theoretically claim to differ from situationism, in actual practice the *method* used to arrive at moral decisions would be similar. The differences between the two views should not bind us to their resemblances; in both cases man decides what is moral and what is not.

Universal Norms

The Bible presents a moral system which has universal validity. This does not mean that moral decisions are always easy to make, since there may be legitimate disagreements as to whether a given act falls under the universal norm. Is a lie merely a false impression? Is gambling stealing? Is abortion murder? These are legitimate subjects for discussion and even disagreement. But whenever an action clearly falls under a propositional command of Scripture, that command judges the action as moral or immoral *without* exception.

It is difficult to predict what a Christian might do if faced with the decision of lying or telling the hiding place of friends when an enemy appears at his door, but several observations are pertinent.

First, the moral laws given in the Scripture have *intrinsic* value. Since the commands are a reflection of God's own nature, any infringement of them constitutes sin. Admittedly, no one keeps the commands perfectly, but the objective standard remains the same. If a lie is told, sin has been committed, regardless of the situation. But since the Scriptures judge morality by intentions, a person would not be guilty of lying if he actually thought he was speaking the truth. For example, to say, "The door is open" when one thought it was, would not be sin, even if the door was actually closed. Similarly, we may actually speak the truth and yet be lying. One might make a false statement intending to deceive, but unknown to the speaker, the statement is true. In this case the speaker has lied, that is, sinned, even though through circumstances unknown to him he happened to speak the truth. Since he *thought* he was lying and *intended* to deceive his listener, he is guilty of violating the the biblical command Thou shalt not bear false witness.

Responsibility is therefore based on knowledge. But the point is that whenever one acts with intentions which are contrary to biblical commands, he has sinned. The "good" intention of trying to protect friends does not erase the immoral act of intentionally telling a lie to deceive an enemy. Of course, if faced with the decision of whether to lie or tell the truth, a Christian might lie (who can tell how anyone would react under such tension?); but if a lie has been told, the Christian must come to the cross for forgiveness.§

Second, the Christian contends that if exceptions are made to moral laws, these exceptions must have scriptural authority. Some have erroneously supposed that when Christians approve

§This point is frequently stressed by John Warwick Montgomery (cf. *Christianity Today*, July 21, 1971, p. 8). Montgomery rejects the hierarchical position and holds that scriptural commands have universal validity. None can be intentionally broken without committing sin.

of killing in war or capital punishment, they are then situ-
ists (or possibly hierarchicalists) who make an exception to ..c
commandment Thou shalt not kill. But such reasoning is incorrect. The Ten Commandments are given in Exodus 20, and
in the next chapter *God* makes an exception and gives special
instructions as to when capital punishment *is* permissible (Ex
21:12 ff.). Similarly, the question of war must be settled from
the Scriptures. The Christian believes that the only legitimate
exceptions to any command must be based on the revealed
will of God. If one is convinced the Scriptures teach that
capital punishment is to be used by civil leaders and that
killing in war is permissible, this is not situation ethics. God
is the Legislator and is able to permit exceptions to the rules
He has given.

Third, the majority of genuine moral conflicts arise because
of previous sinful actions. A man may foolishly vow to kill
another man. Now he is forced either to break his promise or
become a murderer. In either case he is sinning. Here he must
choose between the lesser of two evils. Hopefully, he will
choose to break his vow. But he would not have been in this
moral dilemma if he had not broken the scriptural instructions
regarding vows (Ec 5:5). Having violated one instruction, he
became entangled and therefore *had* to sin. In this case two
universals were clearly in conflict, but only because one universal had already been broken. Many other similar illustrations
could be given where an individual had to sin, but ideally such
situations need not occur—and in most cases *would* not occur
—if no universals were previously broken.

Fourth, some evils are greater than others. Christians who
think that all sins are equal in the sight of God ignore the plain
teaching of Scripture. (Reference has already been made to
Christ's words about the weightier matters of the law.) Christ
clearly stated that there are degrees of anger and corresponding
degrees of judgment (Mt 5:21-23). And although Christ
taught that looking at a woman to lust was committing adultery,

and hating your brother makes you a murderer, this does not lead us to the conclusion that the thought of the heart is in every respect equal to the act. Judicially in the sight of God the evil thought must be forgiven just as the actual deed, but in terms of their effects, the two are not equal. Sins of the mind do not affect others unless the *act* is committed. In the acts of murder and adultery, the lives of others are being destroyed and ruined: this is not true if one has murderous or adulterous thoughts.

Therefore, if we are faced with a choice between evils, we should evaluate which one is the lesser evil and choose to do the one that will do the least amount of harm. This may involve breaking a vow (as in the illustration above), or telling a lie, stealing, and so on. However, such decisions in which only evil is possible are extremely rare. As previously noted, such entanglements are usually the result of previous sins. In the vast majority of difficult situations, evil is *not* a necessity. But whenever a commandment has been intentionally broken, a sin has been committed.

Fifth, since morality is based on intentions, we are not responsible for fulfilling scriptural obligations if we are incapable of doing so. For example, the Scriptures teach that a man should provide for his family. But what if he should be in an accident and be crippled for life? In such instances he is not to be held morally guilty of breaking God's instructions. This view has further implications. Just as one who is physically unable to fulfill God's obligations is not guilty of breaking God's instructions, likewise those who are morally unable to fulfill the commandments are not guilty. When Mrs. Bergmeier was in the Russian prison camp, she had the option of committing adultery and then going home (if the scheme worked—and evidently in this case it did) or staying under the control of her captors. Some think that this means that she was faced with a decision that involved two conflicting moral principles, namely, the duty to take care of her family and marital fidelity. Geisler suggests that if one takes the position that both of these principles should not be broken, "then she should painfully submit to the lesser of two evils and ask God to forgive her breach of marital fidelity (i.e., assuming that duty to her family was the greater good)."[19] But Mrs. Bergmeier does not have to choose between two evils. If she stays in prison she is not held responsible for failing to take care of her family. Since the Scriptures clearly forbid doing evil that good might come, she is not free to commit adultery without incurring guilt. Through a situation beyond her control she was placed in a position where she could not fulfill the duty to her family. She is not therefore in a position where she *must* sin.

What is true of Mrs. Bergmeier is true of others. Should a girl seduce men for her country for purposes of espionage? Since such action would again violate God's prohibition of adultery, the girl is not responsible for her country if she decides to obey the seventh commandment and live in sexual purity. Perhaps this is the answer to Geisler's criticism of the absolutist's view, namely, that "it inconsistently holds that one is held responsible for not doing good when only evils are possible."[20] But in the vast majority of instances, evil is not the only alternative. If we refuse to break one of the commandments, we are not responsible for the results.

Sixth, since God is sovereign, He is able to control the consequences. This fact is rejected by situationism and underplayed by hierarchicalism. When Joseph Fletcher was at the Religio-Medical Conference in Chicago on February 9, 1972, he said that situationism is frequently accused of playing God. His response was that it does indeed play God, but he added that the word *God* needed redefining. He said that the traditional, that is, personal God has been dying by inches and is already dead. What remains now is only the God of the gaps. However, Fletcher errs in assuming that God is not personal. He always has and will continue to control the affairs of men. Since He keeps the books, it is our responsibility to keep His commandments and let the chips fall where they may.

If situationism or hierarchicalism would be the ethical philosophy of the New Testament, there would be no Christian martyrs. Since both theories permit lying if higher norms or values are at stake, the martyrs would have decided that a lie, that is, denying to be a Christian, is indeed a small price to pay to save a life. The superior duty of faithfulness to the family would vitiate the lower norm of truth-telling. But martyrdom is commended in the New Testament because a martyr has proved that he will not do evil; that is, falsify his true identity that good may come. If he and his friends die, God is in control of such consequences. Daniel did not *pretend* that he did not have faith in God when he was told to stop praying to his God. Yet, in this instance God spared his life by a direct miracle. In an equally miraculous way, the lives of his three friends were spared when they refused to bow to the image. The Christian believes that his responsibility is obedience and that the consequences of moral action are then in the hands of God. If refusing to commit adultery or even telling the truth (if there are no scriptural alternatives) causes others to die, this also is within the providence of God. Surely the God of the Scriptures is not one whose plans for certain individuals are frustrated because someone told the truth. If He wants to spare the lives of some, He has the right; if wicked men kill others, neither He nor those who lived within the commands of Scripture are blameworthy. We play the game; God keeps the score.

Seventh, the Christian considers Christ's obedience to the Father (which included obedience to the moral precepts of the Old Testament) as the ethical ideal. He was obedient unto death and yet did not sin. Earlier in this book we gave evidence to show that Christ was not a situationist (as defined in Fletcherian terms). But a final problem remains. Did He adhere to a hierarchical view of morality and therefore break (transcend) the lower norms in favor of the higher?

Geisler thinks that the life of Christ is the most telling objection to the absolutist's view (i.e., the position adopted in this book). He says that if absolutism would be correct, "it would render the sinlessness of Christ either impossible or meaningless as a paradigm of Christian morality."[21] The logic behind this statement is that if there are certain situations in which sin is inevitable, then surely Christ faced them. If He did not face them, the fact that He did not sin would be quite meaningless; if He did face them, then (according to the absolutist) He was in a position where He had to sin. Geisler sees the solution to this dilemma in hierarchicalism. Since Christ was tempted in all points as we are, He encountered the same tragic situations that we face. But when faced with choices where doing evil (according to the absolutist) was a necessity, He simply chose to "transcend" the lower obligation in favor of the higher. In doing this He would have been "exempt" from the lower norm and hence would still be without sin.

This view of Christ's obedience involves two fallacies. To begin with, there is no scriptural evidence that Christ broke or "transcended" *any* of the commandments. Admittedly, we do not have a record of all of the decisions and activities of Christ's life, but it is somewhat perilous to speculate about what He *must* have done. Nothing should be read into the scriptural record to satisfy a given theory. Since Christ's own testimony was always that of obedience to commandments, it is difficult to suppose that He sometimes "transcended" them for one reason or another (Jn 12:49, 15:10). We can hardly imagine that Christ would engage in adultery or lying if the life of someone was at stake. Yet, that is precisely what hierarchicalism would require. Since He was tempted as we are, and since He always chose to break the lower norm, it would follow that He frequently disobeyed the basic commandments of Scripture. But if such a position is accepted, it would be necessary to provide at least one or two clear illustrations of His breaking (transcending) a moral absolute. Until such evidence is presented, Christ should not be presented as a hierarchicalist.

The other difficulty with the hierarchical view of Christ's life is that it is based on the assumption that Christ faced situations in which He had to choose between two evils; that is, situations in which according to the absolutist view He *had* to sin. Previously we noted that there are indeed such situations, but only because some other commandment was already broken prior to the situation. But if a commandment is not broken in the first place, one is not forced to choose the lesser of two evils. Furthermore, Christ was not responsible for obligations which could only be fulfilled by breaking moral precepts (cf. point five above).

He was indeed tempted in all points as we are. Satan tried to get Him to respond to basic human weaknesses; He was rejected by His foes and deserted by His followers. He even went through death (which is the dominant theme of Heb 2:14-18), but in all of these situations He obeyed the Father perfectly. Since the commands are the will of God, neither Christ nor His followers are forced to break them in order to gain the Father's approval.

Finally, the moral conflicts we face should not be used as evidence that the commands of Scripture are not universals (situationism) nor that they can sometimes be transcended without sin (hierarchicalism). Both of these views are attractive primarily because they claim to find a satisfactory solution to unusual ethical problems. If moral laws are rooted in the nature of God, they are binding for all time. Given the limitations of human knowledge and the sinfulness of human nature, moral failures and conflicts should serve as a reminder that we cannot be acceptable to God in ourselves. Rather than relaxing God's requirements, we must see His demands as having been met in Christ. Certainly we are able to meet the basic moral requirements outwardly, but since God looks on the heart, such external obedience is not sufficient. For this reason the Scriptures teach that all men have sinned and come short of God's glory, that is, God's standard. But this fact is not a reason for despair. There is another side to the coin. Those who believe on Christ are credited with His righteousness, and in this way God's requirements can be fully met by us all. "Him who knew no sin he made to be sin on our behalf; that we might become the righteousness of God in him" (2 Co 5:21, ASV).

Conclusion: Bridging the Gap?

HISTORY DOES NOT MOVE in isolated segments. Each generation is influenced by the one which preceded it, and it in turn shapes the one which follows. But this raises a question: What accounts for the present emphasis on moral freedom, permissiveness, and relativism? The establishment, which is primarily the older members of the middle class, watches incredulously as the new generation takes its drug trips, bombs buildings, and organizes nude demonstrations. Sometimes it is hard to believe that these two generations were reared in the same world. What accounts for this gap in moral conduct?

Simply to point a finger at one segment of society as though it exists in isolation from the whole is insufficient. The older generation which has been so quick to criticize the new avantgarde approach of relativity in morals has forgotten that the present is influenced by the past. In short, the good old days laid the foundation for the bad new days.

There was a time in American history when the Scriptures were widely regarded as authoritative in matters of religion and morals. Most of the people thought in terms of absolutes; some actions were invariably wrong, others were regarded as right. Those who overstepped the bounds of moral conduct were duly punished. Puritanism, which today has a stigma it does not fully deserve, had strict moral codes which were rigidly enforced. Obviously there was not always unanimous agreement regarding moral issues, but the primary moral laws

114

were generally accepted. But as religious liberalism begaɪ attack on the Scriptures, and as philosophers rejected the doctrine of a personal God, man became depersonalized; he was regarded simply as a machine, the product of time plus chance.

Without a word from outside the universe, man was cast out on a sea without a shore. Secular existentialism reminded him of the despair and futility which were to be his legacy. Such a philosophy has been widely propounded by philosophers, books, and movies which teach that there is no truth, no meaning, no absolute.

The older generation has not felt this influence. They keep thinking of the good old days when moral codes were accepted, truth was upheld, and modesty was a virtue. But tragically, much of the older middle class society has also rejected the Scriptures as the revelation of a personal God. Therefore they have no basis for the values which they have inherited from the days when biblical Christianity was in vogue. This is why Francis Schaeffer states that such people simply function on a "memory," and adds,

> This is why so many young people feel that the middle class is ugly. These people are plastic, ugly and plastic because they try to tell others what to do on the basis of their own values, but with no ground for those values. They have no base and they have no categories.[1]

What this older generation does not understand is that if the Scriptures are not authoritative, then the younger generation is perfectly correct in pushing human ethics to its ultimate conclusion. If man is left to define his own ethics, why should students not have others do their term papers and even advertise for recruits on the university bulletin boards? Why should pornography not be sold in university bookstores? Why should coeducational dormitories be forbidden? Why should wife-swapping clubs not be encouraged? Or why should marriage itself not be considered out of date? Why should nude demonstrations be banned? Why should homosexuality be considered abnormal? Why should university or government buildings not be bombed? Why anything?

When moral dilemmas arise, the reaction of those who have rejected absolutes is pathetic. University professors ask their students not to cheat even though they cannot tell them why they shouldn't. Or if they do, the reasons are usually trivial; such as, "You will fail"; or "It's important that you learn to do research." Parents don't want their children to participate in sex orgies, but when their children ask why, the best they can do is plead, "Think of what our friends will say. You are ruining our family reputation." But if the child does not care whether he knows how to do research and cares even less about what the friends of the family think, he has no reason to follow traditional moral codes. The fault lies not merely with the children, but with the older generation that looks with nostalgia to the days when moral values were highly regarded, although they themselves have lost the basis of the values they had inherited. Francis Schaeffer tells the story of John Gardner, head of the Urban Coalition, who gave a lecture on restoring values to our culture. When he was asked on what he based his values, he could only look down and say, "I do not know."[2]

There is no reason for this older generation's bewilderment in asking, "What is this world coming to?" It is simply arriving at the destination made inevitable by a preceding generation that rejected the Scriptures as a revelation from a personal God. The younger set, in its quest for answers, has simply been more consistent in its moral philosophy: If there is no God, no absolute, no meaning, why should the traditions of the past be accepted? Why not let morality simply become a matter of personal preference?

Joseph Fletcher has attempted to give ethical answers apart from divine revelation. One of the reasons for the success of his writings is that he articulated a viewpoint which had already been widely accepted in practice. The only reason his ethical philosophy has not brought total chaos to the moral scene is that this nation is still living on the Christian legacy it inherited from its more religious founders.* Thus situationism has come to coexist with at least some semblance of absolutes. For example, some politicians still accuse their opponents of dishonesty and thereby imply (contrary to Fletcher) that truth has some inherent value. Stealing and murder are usually regarded as immoral, even if the culprit had good intentions or if he acted to achieve a "good" end.

However, unless there is some mass return to scriptural authority, the future can be predicted with some measure of accuracy. The generations which follow will probably be more consistent than the present generation which has clung to some absolutes but without any justification. Presumably such vestigial moral remains will be gone in the future. Situationism will be consistently applied. That which was formerly classified as good can then be considered evil, previous evil can be regarded as good, everyone will be permitted to do whatever seems right in his own eyes, and chaos will prevail.

If we wish to stop this moral toboggan slide, we cannot merely reiterate the need for moral absolutes because of the reverence attributed to past traditions. Our plan of attack must be more basic. First, the Scriptures must be proclaimed as an authoritative revelation from a sovereign God who pronounces judgment on those who regard evil as good and good as evil (Is 5:20). The biblical doctrines of sin, judgment, and salvation must once again be heard with clarity and power. As individuals come to trust Christ personally, the Holy Spirit will give them the power necessary to live righteously. Second,

---

*Of course some forms of biblical morality are practiced in nonchristian countries. The apostle Paul wrote that those who have not the law but yet do it, show that the law is written in their hearts (Ro 2:15). But in such instances, moral values originate from intuition and are not the product of philosophical demonstration. However, if moral values are derived solely from human reason, even the most basic moral codes—honesty, prohibitions against stealing, murder, etc.— can be rejected as inherently valuable, as Joseph Fletcher gladly ackowledges. Logically such a view leads to chaos. Morality becomes a matter of personal preference.

coupled with this proclamation, those who know Christ must live lives that properly exemplify Christian conduct. Logically, Christianity could be true even if no one lived the Christian life; but in practice, few people believe unless Christians themselves live lives beyond reproach. As Christ put it, His followers are to let their lights shine in such a way that the world might see their good works and glorify their Father who is in heaven (Mt 5:16).

Fortunately, a growing number of individuals of all ages have determined not to adopt an ethic based on relativistic human values. Many, like the prophet Daniel, have determined not to defile themselves with the social values of their generation. Deep personal commitment is needed to withstand the pressures of our permissive society, and such commitment is not optional. If the choice is (as it appears to be) between a return to biblical morality or the acceptance of consistent situationism, the people of this nation must make a crucial decision—a decision which cannot be postponed indefinitely. We must either return to a biblically rooted moral ethic, or learn to accept without rebuke legalism, rioting, bombings, stealing, murder, sexual perversion, and despair. If the Christians in America decide to bridge the morality gap by a return to biblical morality, it will be a long trip back. May God help us to take that first big step.

Notes

1

1. *U.S. News and World Report,* February 1, 1971, p. 27.
2. Ibid., January 18, 1971, p. 13.
3. *The Challenge of Crime In A Free Society* (Washington: U.S. Government Printing Office, 1967), p. 32.
4. *Chicago Tribune,* August 23, 1970.
5. Ibid.
6. Pierre Burton, *The Comfortable Pew* (Winnipeg: Universal Printers, 1965), p. 63.
7. Ibid.

2

1. Joseph Fletcher, *Situation Ethics* (Philadelphia: Westminster, 1966), pp. 164-65.
2. Ibid., p. 18.
3. Ibid., p. 23.
4. Ibid., p. 26.
5. John A. T. Robinson, *Honest To God* (Philadelphia: Westminster, 1963), p. 112.
6. Fletcher, p. 30.

3

1. Joseph Fletcher, *Situation Ethics,* p. 58.
2. Ibid.
3. Ibid., p. 125.
4. Ibid., p. 61.
5. Gordon H. Clark, *A Christian View of Men and Things* (Grand Rapids: Eerdmans, 1951), p. 188.
6. Peter Abelard, *Abailard's Ethics* (Oxford: Basil Blackwell, 1935), p. 29.
7. Ibid., p. 55.
8. Fletcher, "Reflection and Reply," *The Situation Ethics Debate,* ed. Harvey Cox (Philadelphia: Westminster, 1968), p. 257.
9. Fletcher, *Situation Ethics,* p. 61.
10. Ibid., p. 59.
11. Ibid., p. 42.
12. Ibid., p. 14.
13. Ibid., p. 125.
14. Joseph Fletcher, *Moral Responsibility* (Philadelphia: Westminster, 1968), p. 40.
15. Fletcher, *Situation Ethics,* p. 72.

16. Ibid., p. 151.
17. Robinson, *Honest To God*, p. 115.
18. James M. Gustafson, "How Does Love Reign?" *Christian Century*, May 12, 1966.
19. Fletcher, *Situation Ethics*, p. 95.
20. Jeremy Bentham, *An Introduction to the Principles of Morals and Legislation* rev. (New York: Dolphin Books, Doubleday, 1961), pp. 35-39.
21. Clark, pp. 170-71.
22. Fletcher, *Situation Ethics*, p. 115.
23. Ibid., p. 95.
24. Ibid., p. 96.
25. Joseph Fletcher, "What's in a Rule?: A Situationist's View," *Norm and Context in Christian Ethics*, ed. Gene Outka and Paul Ramsey, (New York: Scribner, 1968), p. 332.
26. Joseph Fletcher, *Moral Responsibility*, p. 23.
27. Fletcher, *Situation Ethics*, p. 121.

4

1. Joseph Fletcher, *Situation Ethics*, p. 55.
2. Ibid., p. 57.
3. Lawrence Richards, "To Do the Loving Thing Manward," *Action* (Spring 1968), p. 23.
4. Fletcher, p. 39.
5. Richards, p. 23.
6. Fletcher, p. 136.
7. Ibid., p. 113.
8. Paul Ramsey, *Deeds and Rules In Christian Ethics* (New York: Scribner, 1967), p. 216.
9. Fletcher, p. 51.
10. Fletcher, "Reflection and Reply," in *The Situation Ethics Debate*, pp. 252-53.
11. Fletcher, *Situation Ethics*, p. 110.
12. Ibid., p. 115.
13. Ibid., pp. 115-16.
14. Ibid., p. 72.
15. Basil Mitchell, "Ideals, Roles, and Rules," in *Norm and Context In Christian Ethics*, ed. Gene Outka and Paul Ramsey (New York: Scribner, 1968), p. 363.
16. Ramsey, p. 190.

5

1. Joseph Fletcher, *Situation Ethics*, p. 136.
2. Fletcher, *Moral Responsibility*, p. 40.
3. George E. Moore, *Principia Ethica* (Great Britain: Cambridge U. Press, 1929), p. 153.
4. Ibid.
5. Fletcher, *Moral Responsibility*, p. 32.
6. Fletcher, *Situation Ethics*, p. 128.
7. Ibid., p. 89.
8. Clark, *A Christian View of Men and Things*, p. 175.
9. Fletcher, *Moral Responsibility*, p. 37.
10. Fletcher, *Situation Ethics*, p. 117.
11. Ibid., p. 118.
12. Ibid., p. 134.

6

1. Joseph Fletcher, *Moral Responsibility*, p. 173.
2. Fletcher, *Situation Ethics*, p. 28.
3. Ibid., p. 39.
4. Ibid., pp. 43-44.
5. Fletcher, *Moral Responsibility*, p. 137.
6. Fletcher, "Reflection and Reply," p. 252.
7. Fletcher, *Situation Ethics*, p. 42.
8. Ibid., p. 129.
9. Ibid.
10. Ibid., p. 148.

7

1. Joseph Fletcher, *Situation Ethics*, p. 140.
2. Fletcher, *Moral Responsibility*, p. 138.
3. *Time*, July 5, 1971, p. 34.
4. Fletcher, *Moral Responsibility*, p. 138.
5. Joseph Fletcher and John Warwick Montgomery, *Situation Ethics: True Or False?* (Minneapolis: Bethany Fellowship, 1972), p. 32.
6. Basil Mitchell, "Ideals, Roles, and Rules," p. 359.
7. Fletcher, *Moral Responsibility*, pp. 151-52.
8. *Chicago Daily News*, February 11, 1971.
9. Fletcher, *Situation Ethics*, p. 49.
10. Ludwig Wittgenstein, "Wittgenstein's Lecture on Ethics," *Philosophical Review*, 74, 1965, p. 7.
11. Ibid.

8

1. Joseph Fletcher, *Situation Ethics*, p. 139.
2. Ibid., p. 69, cf. p. 85.
3. Carl F. Henry, *Christian Personal Ethics* (Grand Rapids: Eerdman's, 1957), p. 314.
4. Ibid.
5. Fletcher, p. 97.
6. Robinson, *Honest To God*, pp. 110-11.
7. Ibid., pp. 109-10.
8. Joseph Fletcher and John Warwick Montgomery, *Situation Ethics: True Or False?*, p. 55.
9. F. Godet, *Commentary on Luke*, 10:27.
10. Fletcher, *Situation Ethics*, p. 126.
11. Ibid., p. 20.
12. John Macquarrie, *Three Issues in Ethics* (New York: Harper & Row, 1970), p. 30.
13. Fletcher, *Situation Ethics*, pp. 126-127.
14. Richard Wurmbrand, *Today's Martyred Church Tortured for Christ* (Great Britain: Hayfield, n.d.), p. 15.

9

1. John Macquarrie, *Three Issues in Ethics*, pp. 39-40.
2. J. P. Mackey, "When Is a Sin Not a Sin?", *U.S. Catholic* (August 1967), p. 16.
3. Joseph Fletcher, *Situation Ethics*, p. 139.

4. Ibid., p. 115.
5. Fletcher, *Moral Responsibility,* p. 19.
6. Norman Geisler, *Ethics: Alternatives and Issues,* (Grand Rapids: Zondervan, 1971), p. 122.
7. Ibid., p. 110.
8. Ibid., p. 125.
9. Ibid., p. 126.
10. Ibid., p. 127.
11. Ibid., p. 115.
12. Ibid., p. 121.
13. Ibid., p. 130.
14. Ibid.
15. Ibid., p. 132.
16. Ibid., p. 131.
17. Ibid., p. 208.
18. Ibid., p. 120.
19. Ibid., p. 106.
20. Ibid., p. 110.
21. Ibid., p. 112.

CONCLUSION

1. Francis A. Schaeffer. *The Church At the End of the 20th Century.* (Downers Grove: Inter-Varsity, 1970), p. 19.
2. Ibid.

Bibliography

BOOKS

Abelard, Peter. *Abailard's Ethics*. Oxford: Basil Blackwell, 1935.

Augsburger, David. *So What? Everybody's Doing It*. Chicago: Moody, 1968.

Banowsky, William S. *The New Morality: A Christian Solution*. Austin: R. B. Sweet, 1968.

Baumgardt, David. *Bentham and the Ethics of Today*. Princeton: Princeton U., 1952.

Bentham, Jeremy. *An Introduction to the Principles of Morals and Legislation*. Rev. Garden City, N.Y.: Doubleday, Dolphin Books, 1961.

Burton, Pierre. *The Comfortable Pew*. Winnipeg: Universal Printers, 1965.

Clark, Gordon H. *A Christian View of Men and Things*. Grand Rapids, Eerdmans, 1952.

————. *Religion, Reason and Revelation*. Nutley, N.J.: Craig, 1961.

————. *Thales To Dewey*. Boston: Houghton Mifflin, 1957.

Cox, Harvey, ed. *The Situation Ethics Debate*. Philadelphia: Westminster, 1968.

Eavey, C. B. *Practical Christian Ethics*. Grand Rapids: Zondervan, 1959.

Fletcher, Joseph. *Moral Responsibility*. Philadelphia: Westminster, 1967.

————. *Situation Ethics*. Philadelphia: Westminster, 1966.

Fletcher, Joseph and Montgomery, John W. *Situation Ethics: True or False?* Minneapolis: Bethany Fellowship, 1972.

Geisler, Norman. *Ethics: Alternatives and Issues.* Grand Rapids: Zondervan, 1971.

Griffiths, Michael D. *Consistent Christianity.* London: Inter-Varsity, 1960.

Hamilton, Kenneth. *What's New in Religion?* Grand Rapids: Eerdmans, 1968.

Harkness, Georgia. *Christian Ethics.* New York: Abingdon, 1967.

Henry, Carl F. H. *Christian Personal Ethics.* Grand Rapids: Eerdmans, 1957.

Macquarrie, John. *Three Issues in Ethics.* New York: Harper & Row, 1970.

Moore, George E. *Principia Ethica.* Great Britain: Cambridge U., 1929.

Murray, John. *Principles of Conduct.* Grand Rapids: Eerdmans, 1964.

Outka, Gene H., and Ramsey, Paul, eds. *Norm and Context in Christian Ethics.* New York: Scribner, 1968.

Redding, David A. *The New Immorality.* Westwood, N.J.: Revell, 1967.

Ridenour, Fritz. *It All Depends.* Glendale, Cal.: Gospel Light, 1969.

Robinson, John A. T. *Honest To God.* Philadelphia: Westminster, 1966.

Saylor, Carlyle L. and Spitzer, Walter O., eds. *Birth Control and the Christian.* Wheaton: Tyndale, 1969.

Schaeffer, Francis A. *Escape From Reason.* London: Inter-Varsity, 1968.

———. *The Church At the End of the 20th Century.* Downers Grove: Inter-Varsity, 1971.

Scudder, C. W., ed. *Crises in Morality.* Nashville: Broadman, 1964.

Snook, John B. *Doing Right and Wrong.* New York: Association, 1966.

Wurmbrand, Richard. *Today's Martyr Church Tortured for Christ.* Great Britain: Hayfield, (n.d.).

PERIODICALS

Brockway, Allan R. Review of *Situation Ethics* by Joseph Fletcher. *Concern,* April 1, 1966.

Editorials. "Don't Surrender God's Absolutes!" *Presbyterian Journal,* February 22, 1967.

Gustafson, James M. "How Does Love Reign?" *Christian Century,* May 12, 1966.

Holmes, Arthur. "New Commandment, New Morality—What's the Difference." *Eternity,* November 1967.

Jeske, Richard L. "Ethical Values Today." *Lutheran Witness,* July 1966.

Kruithof, Bastian. "The Word and Situation Ethics." *Church Herald,* September 9, 1966.

Mackey, J. P. "When Is a Sin Not a Sin?" *U.S. Catholic,* August 1967.

Mehl, Duane. "I Love Because I Love?" *This Day,* December 1966.

Moye, Thomas E. "O Lord, Be Angry With Me." *Pulpit,* January 1968.

Richards, Lawrence O. "To Do the Loving Thing Manward." *Action,* Spring 1968.

Rothwell, Mel-Thomas. "Holiness and A Case in Situation Ethics." *Herald of Holiness,* May 1968.

Sterner, R. Eugene. "Honestly Now!" *Vital Christianity,* October 21, 1968.

"The Bible and the New Morality," *Christianity Today,* July, 1967, pp. 5-9.

Vander Ploeg, John. (Editorials). "Sinai or "Situation Ethics?" *Banner,* June 14, 1968.

Wittgenstein, Ludwig. "Wittgenstein's Lecture on Ethics." *Philosophical Review* 74 (1965).